OLD KEIGHLEY IN PHOTOGRAPHS

By IAN DEWHIRST, B.A., A.L.A.

6

First Edition March 1972
Second Impression October 1974
Third Impression April 1988

Published by: Hendon Publishing Co. Ltd., Hendon Mill, Nelson, Lancashire.

Printed by: Fretwell & Cox Ltd., Goulbourne Street, Keighley, West Yorkshire BD21 1PZ.

Introduction

FOR more than a century and a quarter, the camera has been patiently recording the passage of faces, places and events, clothing with reality a lengthening span of history. If the Victorian photographers, hampered by their bulky equipment and lengthy exposures, had largely to content themselves with empty streets or posed bystanders, they nonetheless managed to freeze for us the texture of their times. Keighley was fortunate, quite early, in its photographers: portrait artists like William Cooke of Strawberry Cottage, outdoor cameramen like John Gill and Walter Tate. The years have brought a sad depletion of their vulnerable glass plates; their prints fade; where, ironically, their pictures survive, the identity of the photographer is often in doubt. Yet a considerable body of their work remains.

The turn of the century onwards saw an increase in the scope and number of photographers, both amateur and professional: Frank Mahoney and F. W. J. Brook, William Edmondson at Haworth, George Crowther of the "Keighley News". My grandfather, Amos Dewhirst, combining photography with a newsagent's shop, was one of several local tradesmen who were producing their own series of picture postcards in the decade prior to the Great War. The vogue for magic lantern shows provided another incentive.

Here, illustrative of a bygone Keighley, is a sample from the wide output of local photographers. The selection, necessarily personal, could not have been compiled without the assistance of Keighley Public Library, the Cliffe Castle Museum and Art Gallery, the "Keighley News", and individual owners of old prints. My special thanks are due to Mr. N. K. Howarth, A.I.B.P., who took my old brown photographs, glass negatives, stereoscopic views and lantern slides—and brought them back to life.

IAN DEWHIRST.

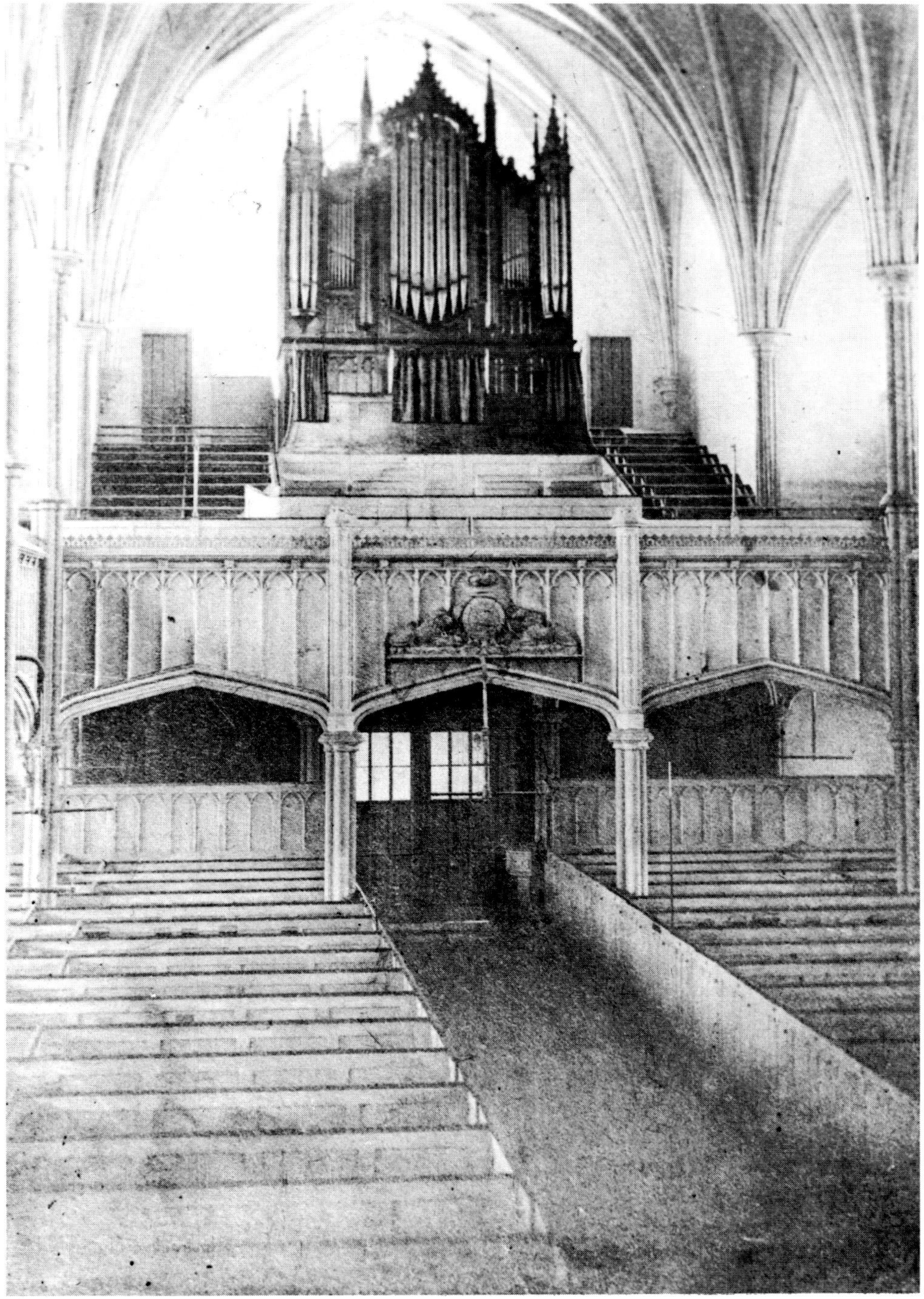

This view, of the west end of the Parish Church demolished in 1846, is possibly the oldest surviving photograph of Keighley. Built in 1805—its hardy predecessor had to be dynamited—the roof was falling in within forty years.

The present Keighley Parish Church was opened in 1848.

An early Haworth photograph: the Black Bull Hotel during the 1850s. Its sign bears the name of William Sugden, innkeeper at the time of the Brontes. On the right, public notices can be discerned fixed to the church gates.

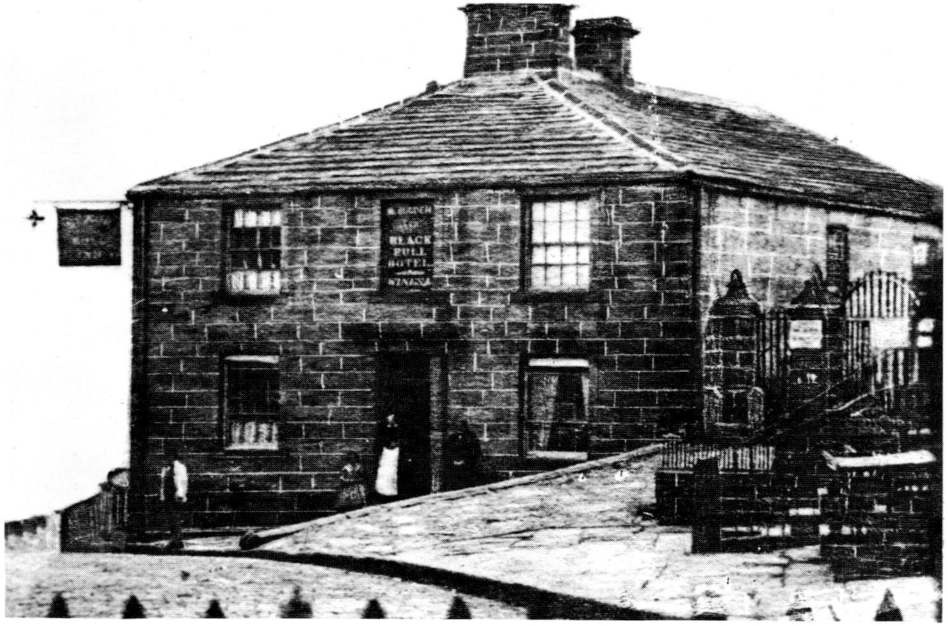

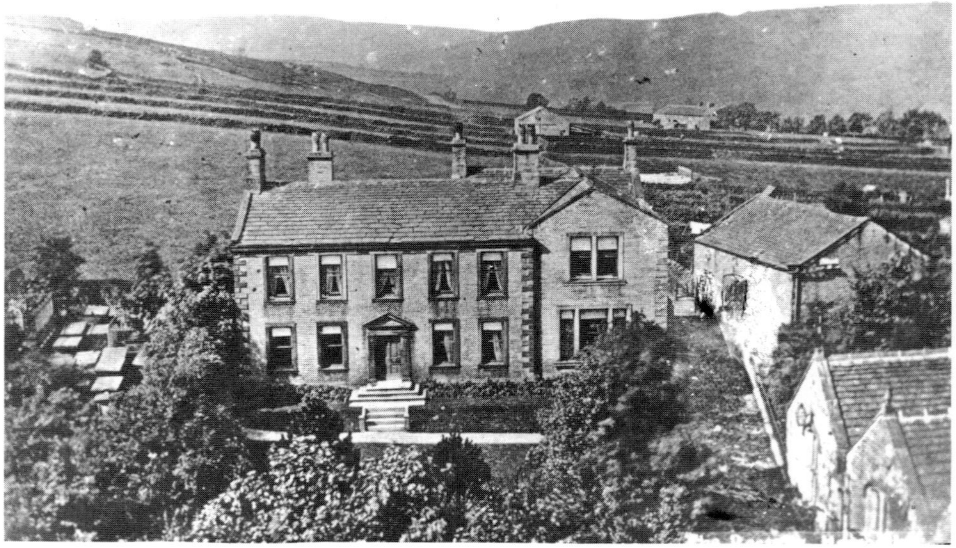

Photographers were quick to take advantage of church towers, as in this aerial view of Haworth's famous Parsonage in 1879, with the Brontes' **ageless path to the moors.**

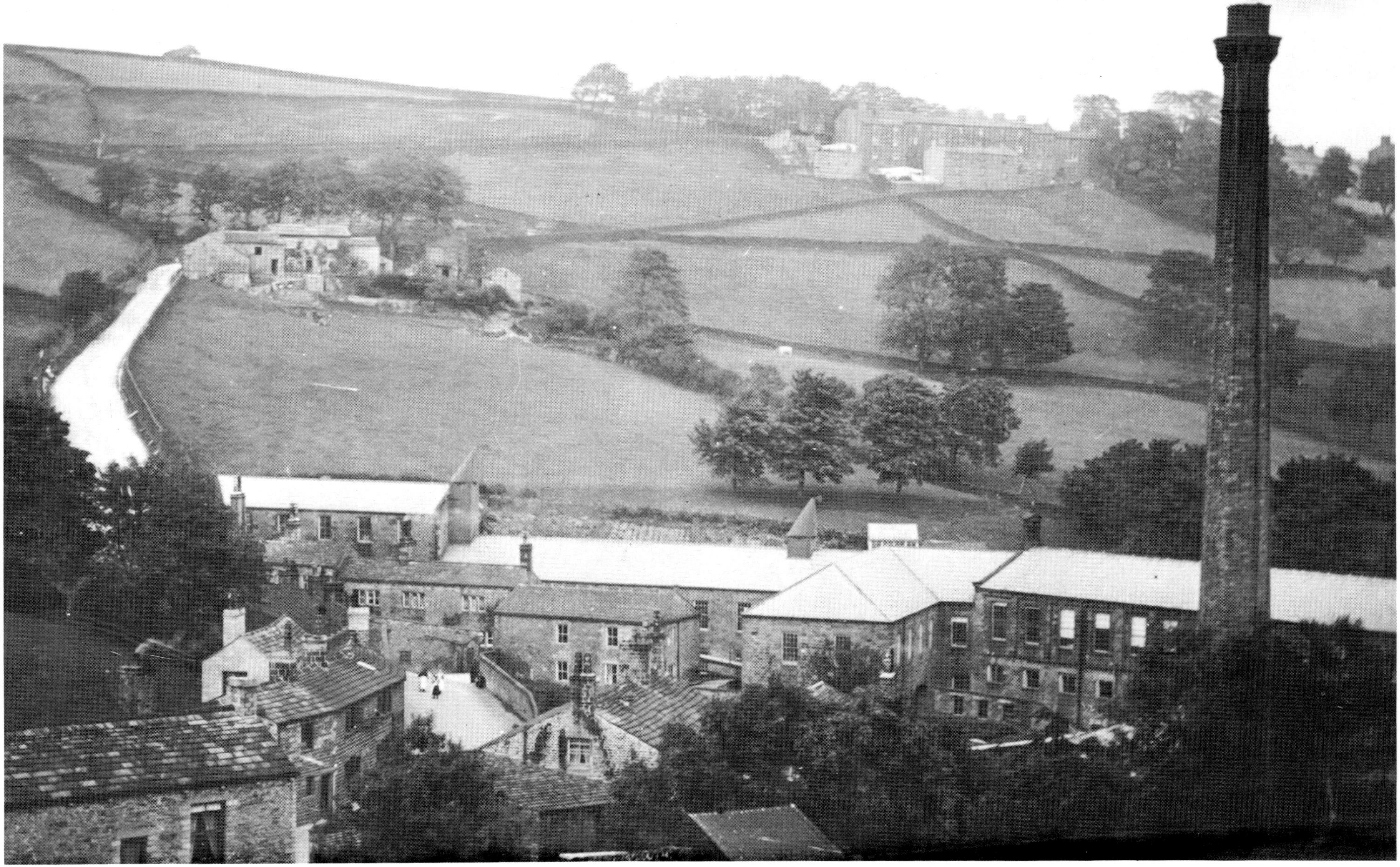

It was the Industrial Revolution, with its demand for water-power, which changed the once-peaceful face of Keighley and its vicinity. Goose Eye, delightfully set in the upper North Beck valley, has been a mill hamlet since the 1790s, first for cotton, then for paper-making. Its rather elegant chimney was demolished in 1970.

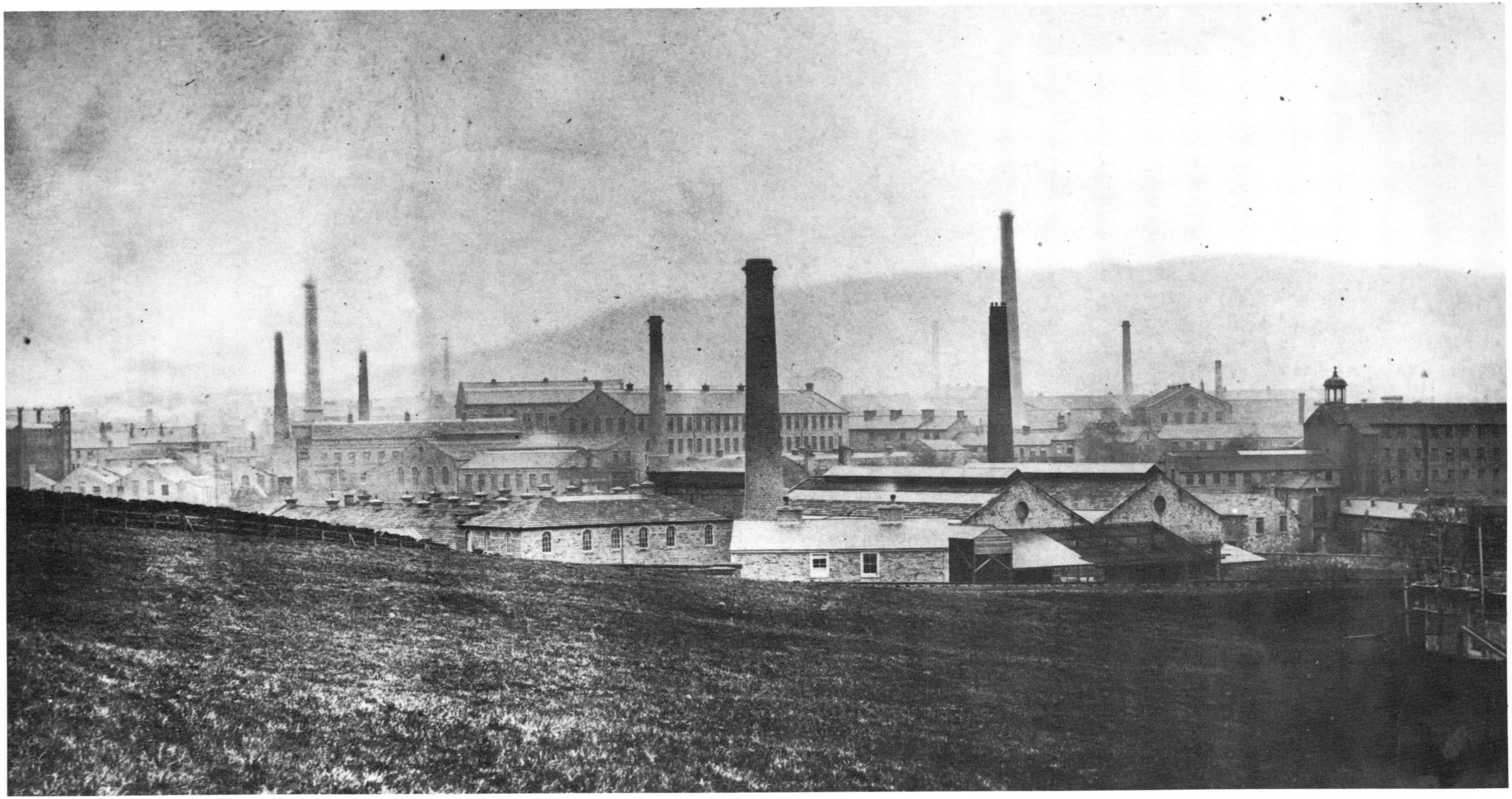

As industry boomed, quiet hamlets became smoky towns—Keighley in the 1870s, viewed from the east. Its population had risen from 5,745 in 1801, to 24,704 in 1871.

By the early nineteenth century, Keighley was a developing worsted town, but smaller craftsmen, too, abounded. Old directories list tinners, cloggers, basket-makers, curriers, nail-makers, saddlers, clockmakers . . . This cooper is working in Chapel Lane.

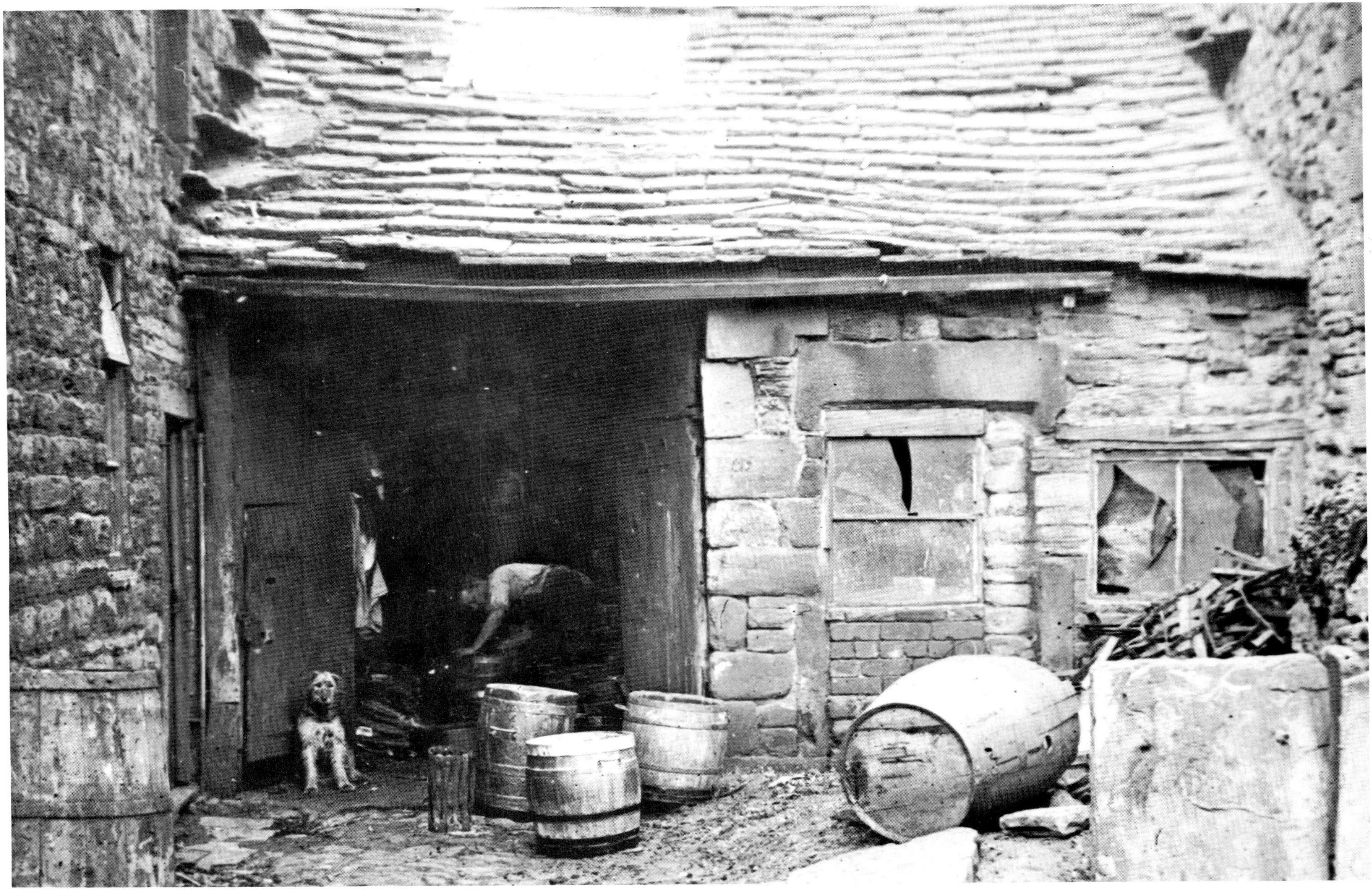

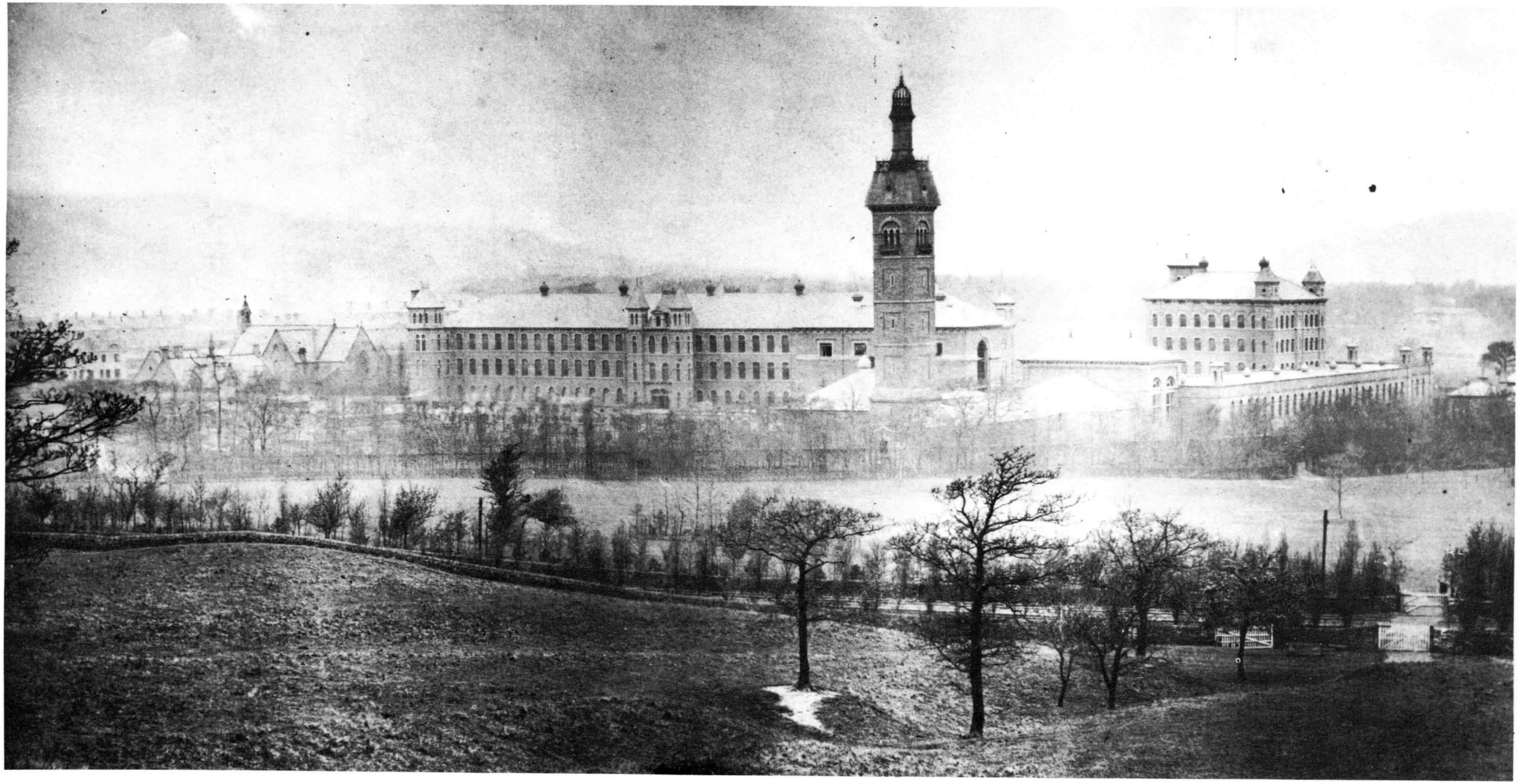

Not all the nineteenth-century mills appeared "dark and satanic". Here, a century ago, the handsome new Dalton Mills—built in 1872—are seen across the Midland Railway line. Industrialist J. H. Craven found a way of compensating for the limited view from his nearby residence at Strong Close: his Dalton Mills chimney was "encircled with a kind of tower, rising nearly as high as the chimney, and from the various points of this tower distant views may be obtained".

Child labour . . . There were early cases of six-year-olds working thirteen hours and more a day, but by 1908 these half-timers, coming out of Haggas's mill, Ingrow, are finishing at noon.

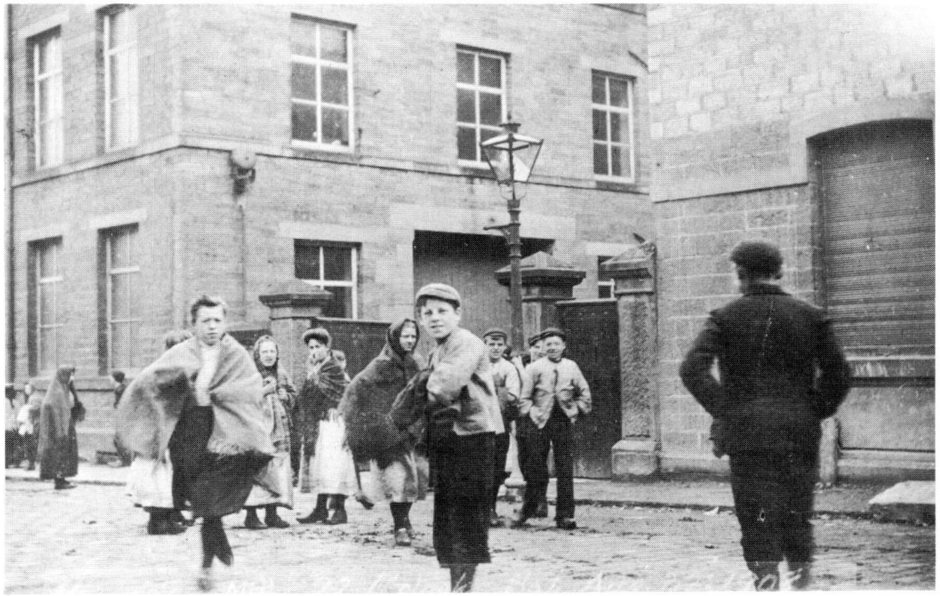

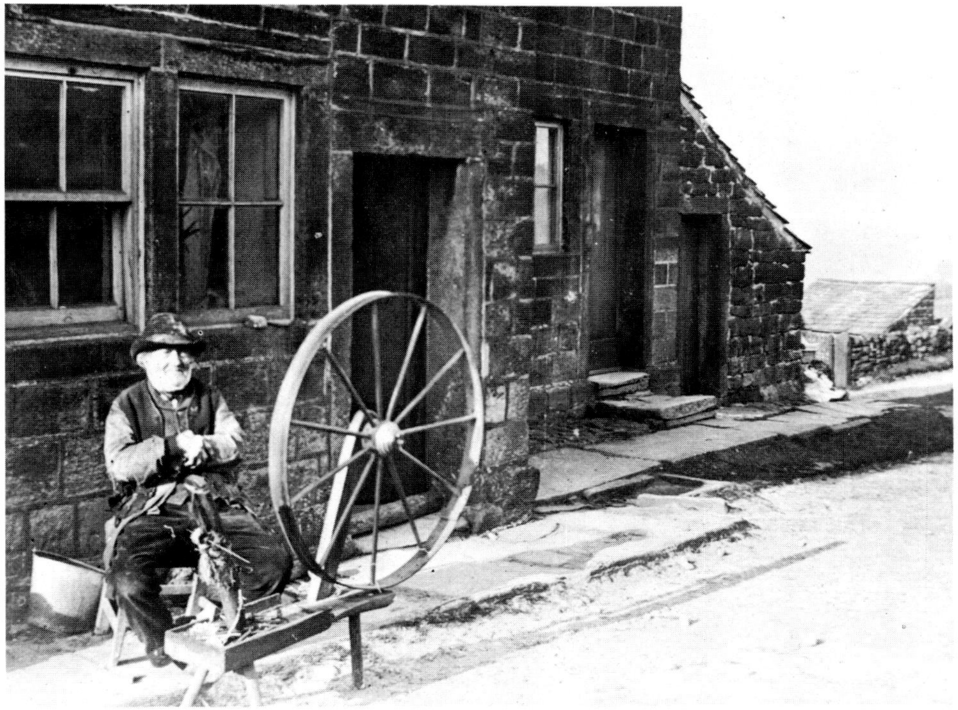

Remnants of an older cottage industry survived the advent of mass-production. Old Timmy Feather, last handloom weaver in the Worth Valley, sits at his bobbin-winder before his home at Buckley Green, Stanbury. Working almost to the end, he died, aged eighty-five, in 1910.

One must look to Keighley's villages for surviving older buildings, such as Laycock's seventeenth-century manor house . .

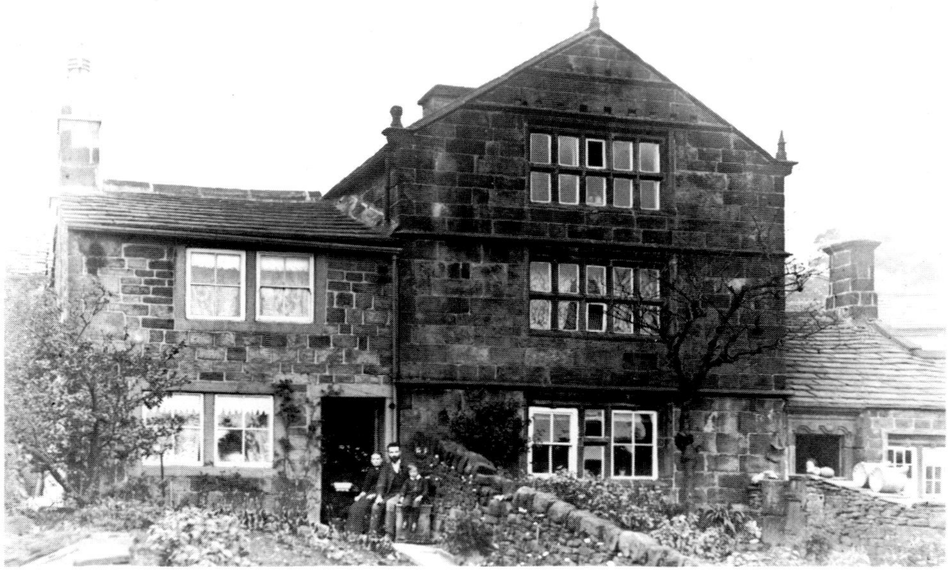

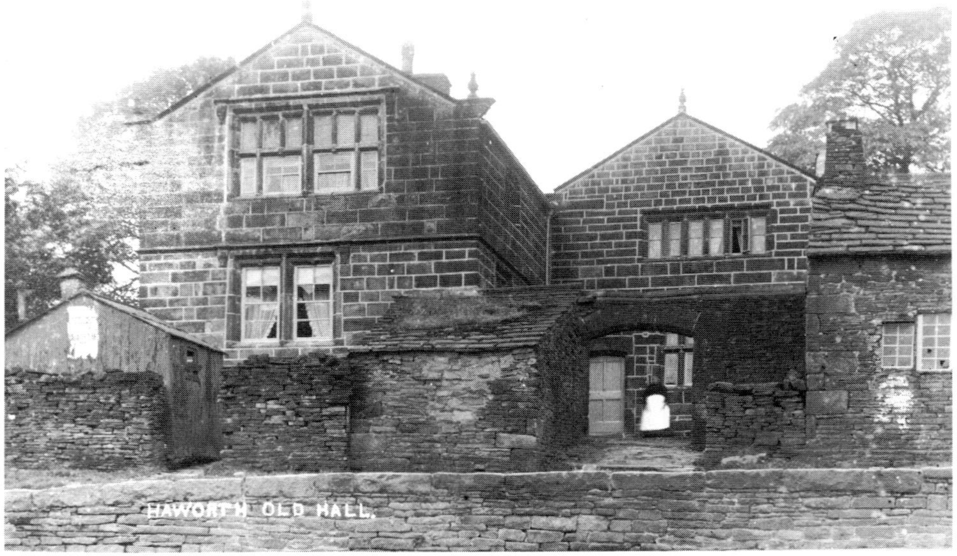

. . . or Haworth's Elizabethan Old Hall, or Emmott Hall, seen here in workaday guise early this century.

It is difficult to equate this pastoral river scene and ivy-clad cottage with modern Stockbridge and its ceaseless traffic. The present bridge was erected in 1930.

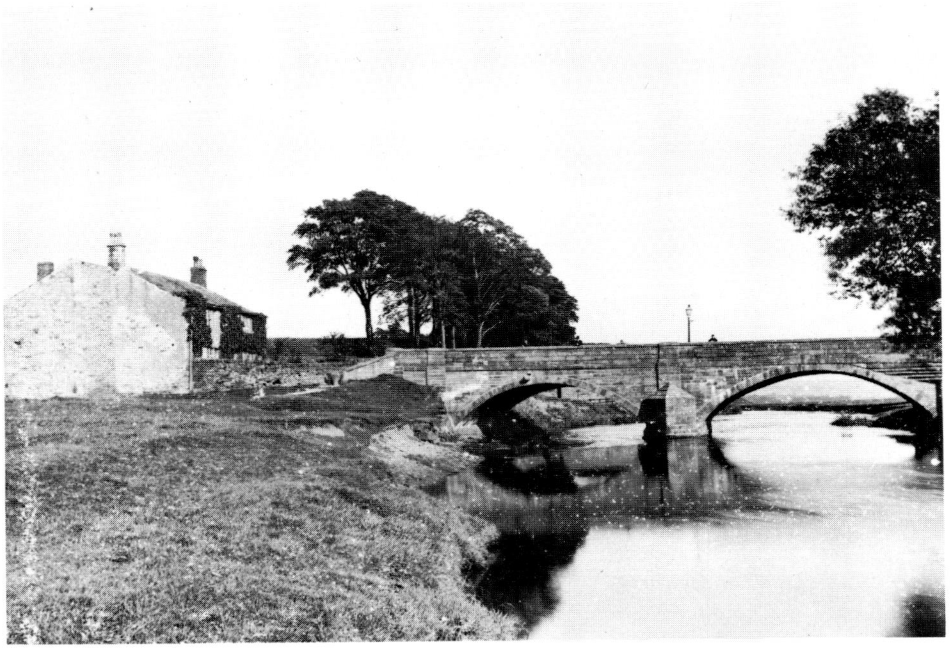

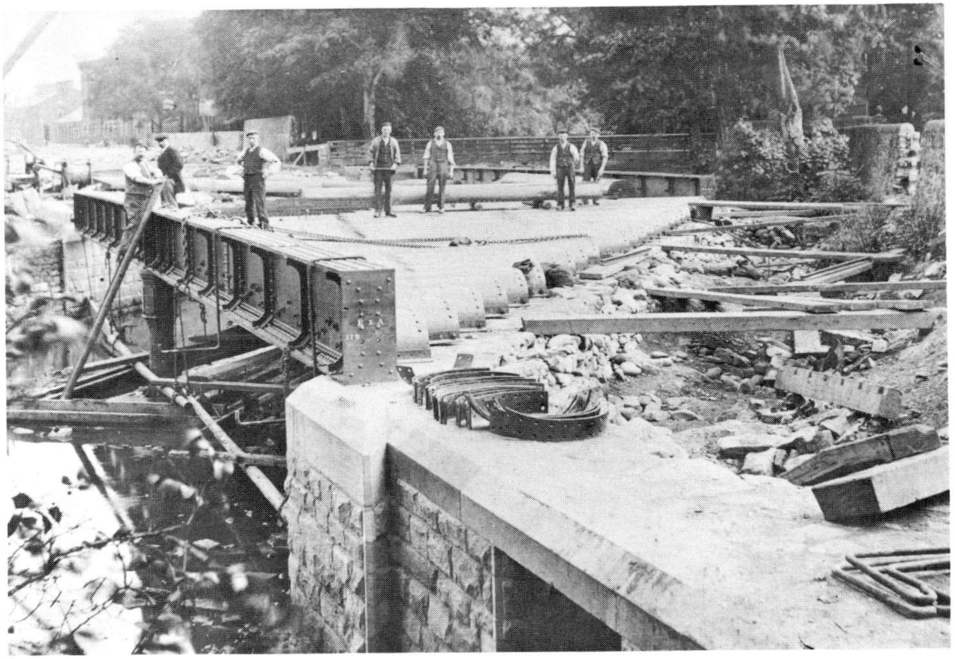

. . . and another rural corner in the act of disappearing: Aireworth Road, previously fording the River Worth, being bridged in 1900. The old wooden footbridge can be seen in the background.

The local stretch of the Leeds-Liverpool Canal was constructed in the 1770s, and by 1819 was sufficiently important for Keighley manufacturers to discuss (to no avail) the addition of a branch canal into the town centre. Here, about 1860, a party of riders prepares to leave the waterside "Marquis of Granby" inn at Riddlesden.

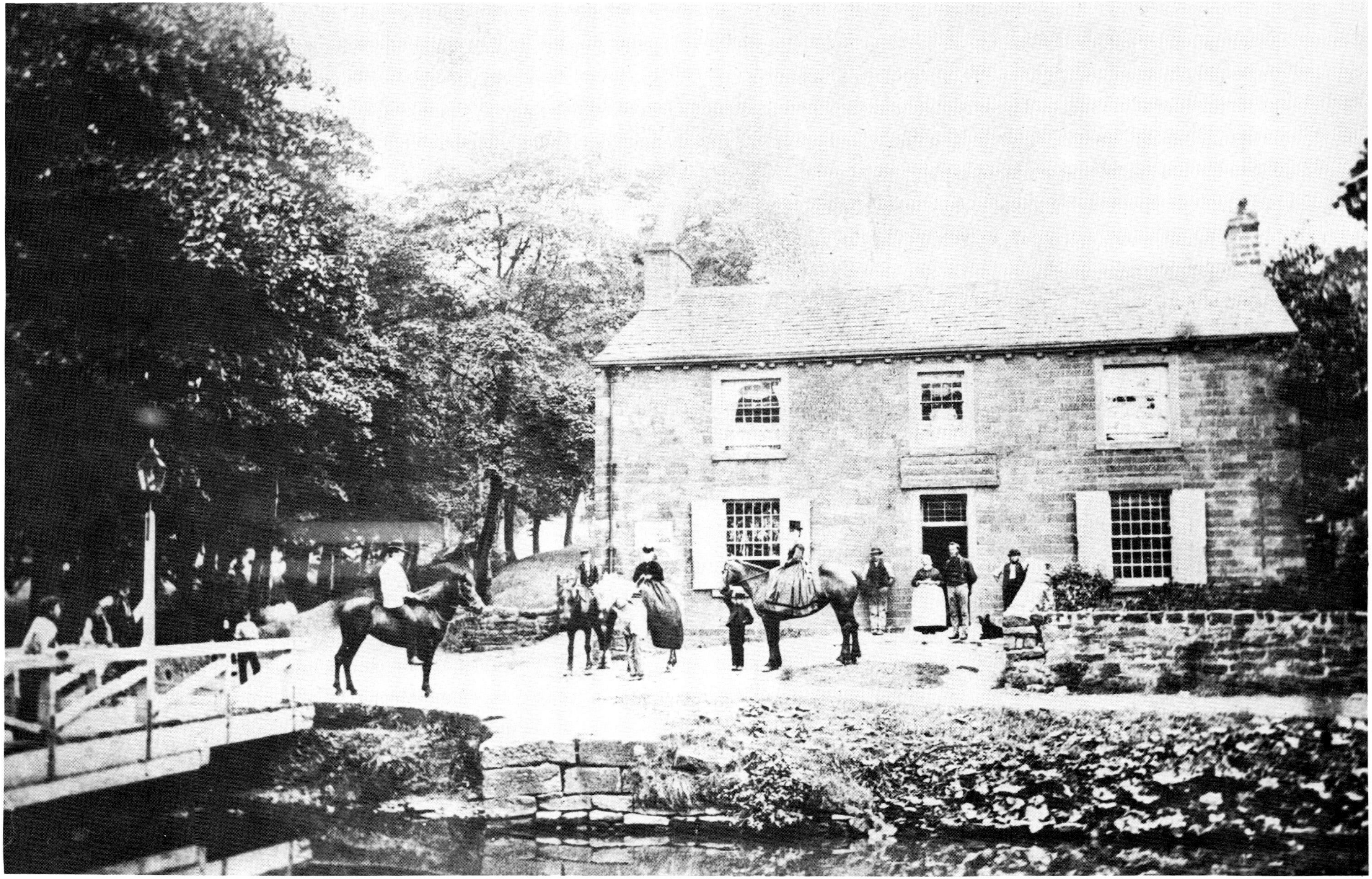

The Railway Age, about 1875. On the right, along the Midland line, a train is approaching Keighley past the Midland Tool Works; to the left, the Worth Valley Railway—opened in 1867—swings out past Low Mill and across the River Worth. The platform was at that time on the farther side of Bradford Road; the present station was built in 1883.

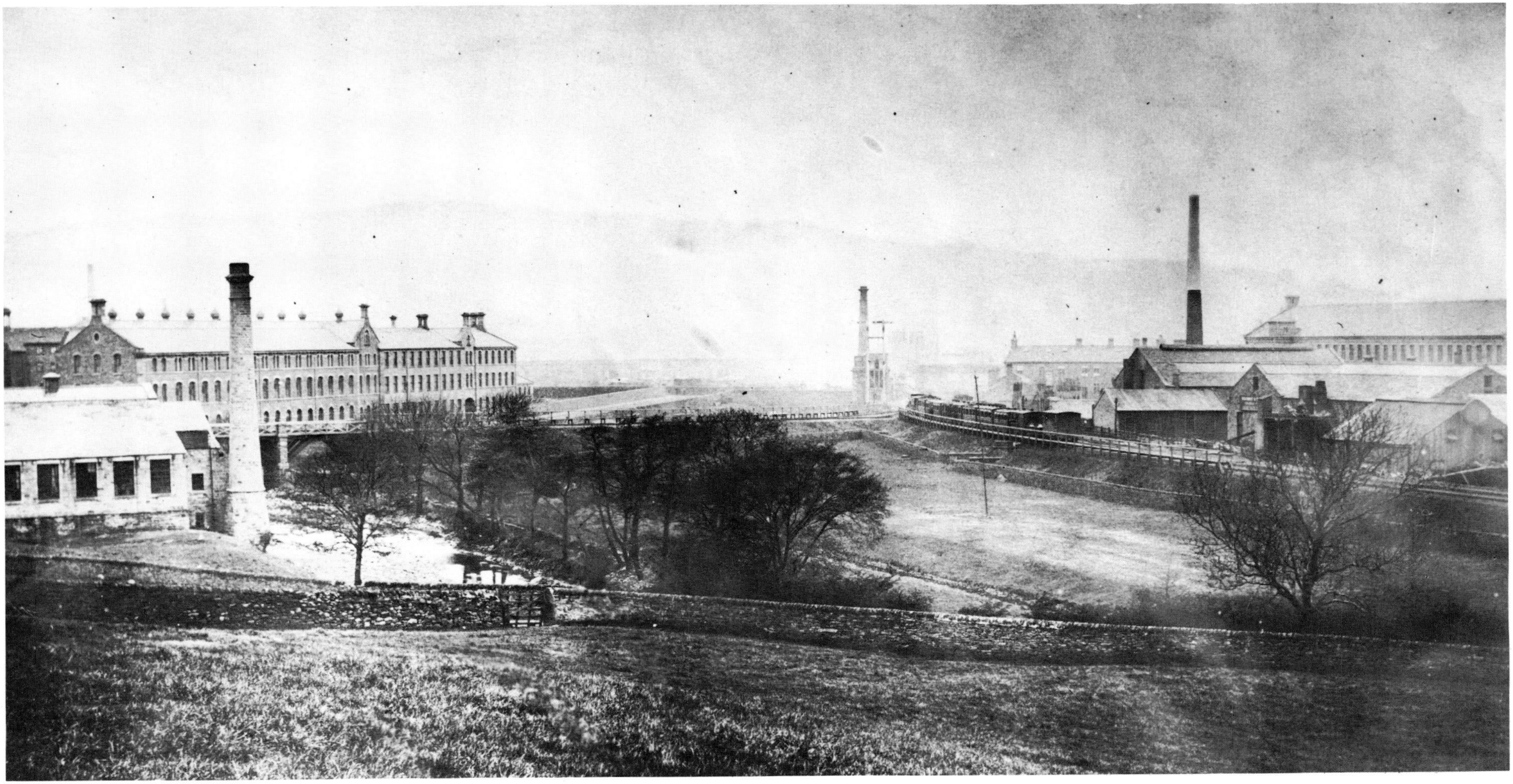

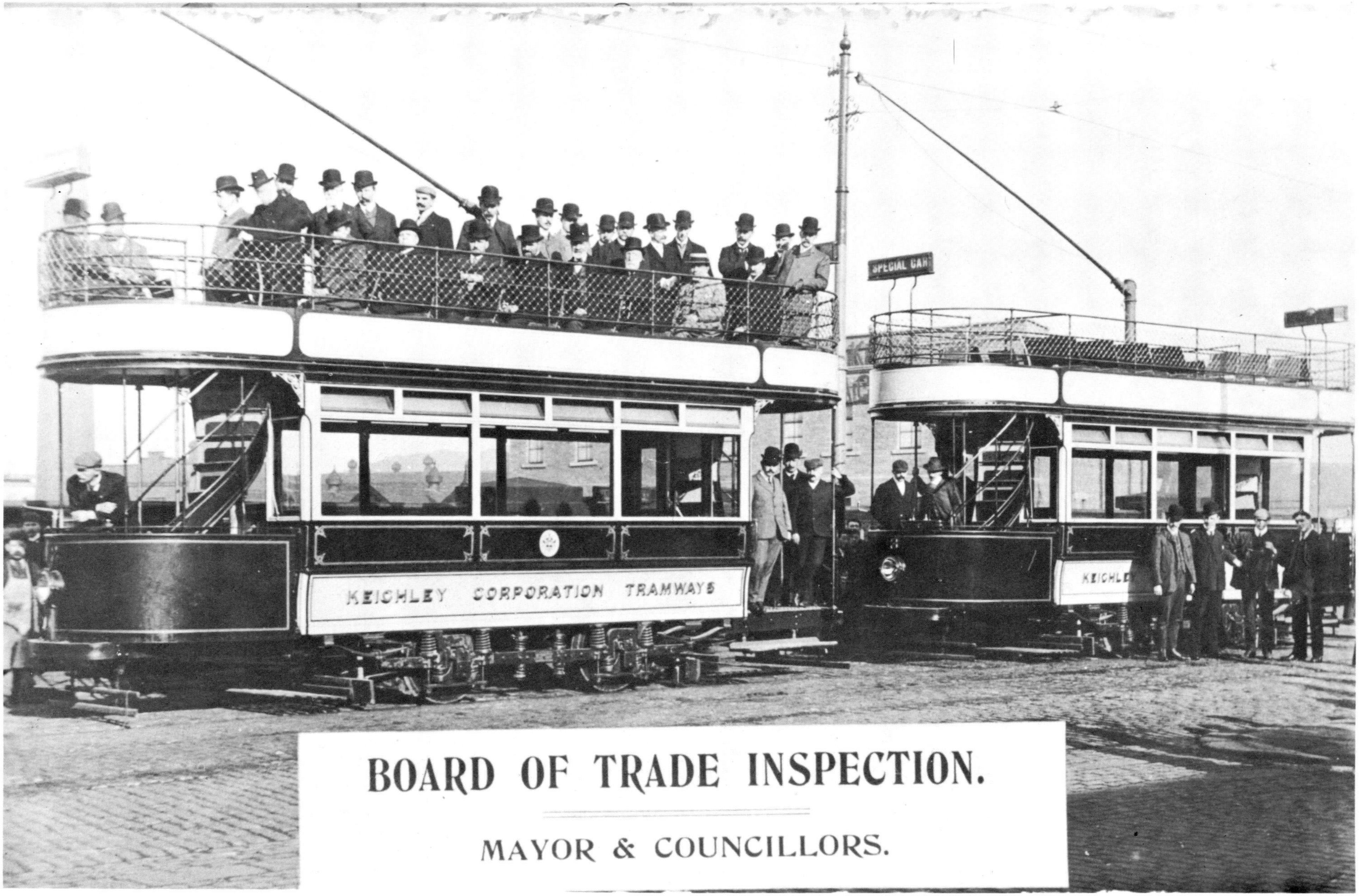

The Board of Trade, the Mayor and Councillors inspect the new electric trams on October 12th, 1904. That same day, 3,589 Keighlians sampled the latest novelty.

A lucky minority of mill-owners—for many went bankrupt—built themselves mansions. Eastwood House was built by William Sugden in 1819. Bought by public subscription in 1891, it served as the Keighley museum from 1899 to 1959.

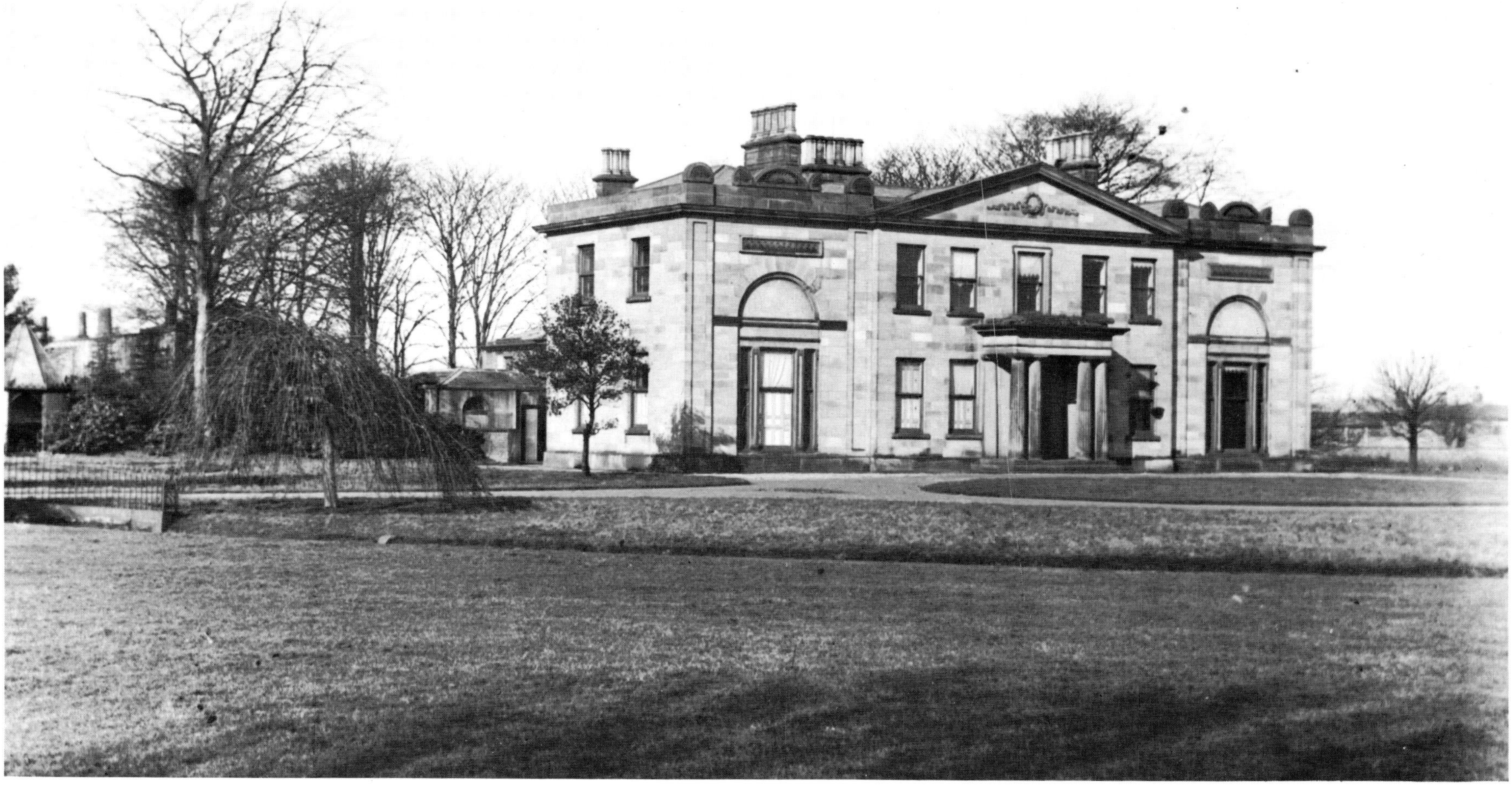

But the most elaborate local mansion was Cliffe Castle. In 1875, on the site of an earlier Cliffe Hall, Henry Isaac Butterfield commenced lengthily building what the "Bradford Illustrated Weekly Telegraph" called "undoubtedly one of the finest residences which have been constructed in Yorkshire, or even the whole Kingdom, during the last decade". Since 1959, shorn of its battlements, it has housed the Cliffe Castle Museum and Art Gallery.

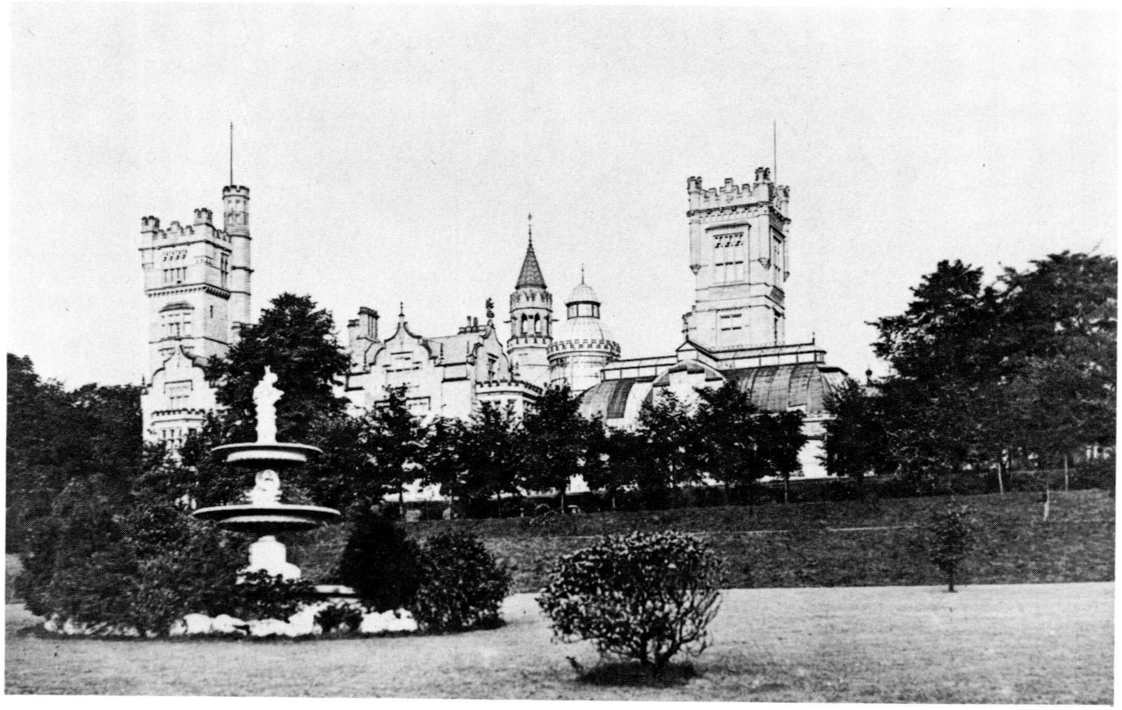

By way of contrast, Keighley's smallest house, in Damside. Its tiny basement was occupied by a dyer.

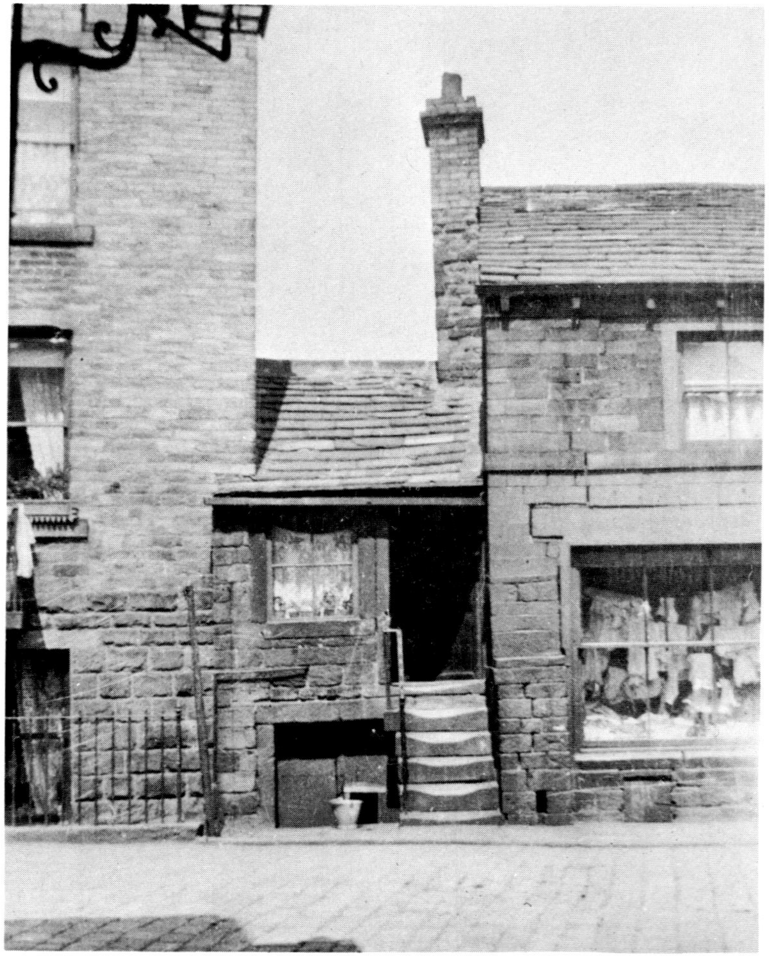

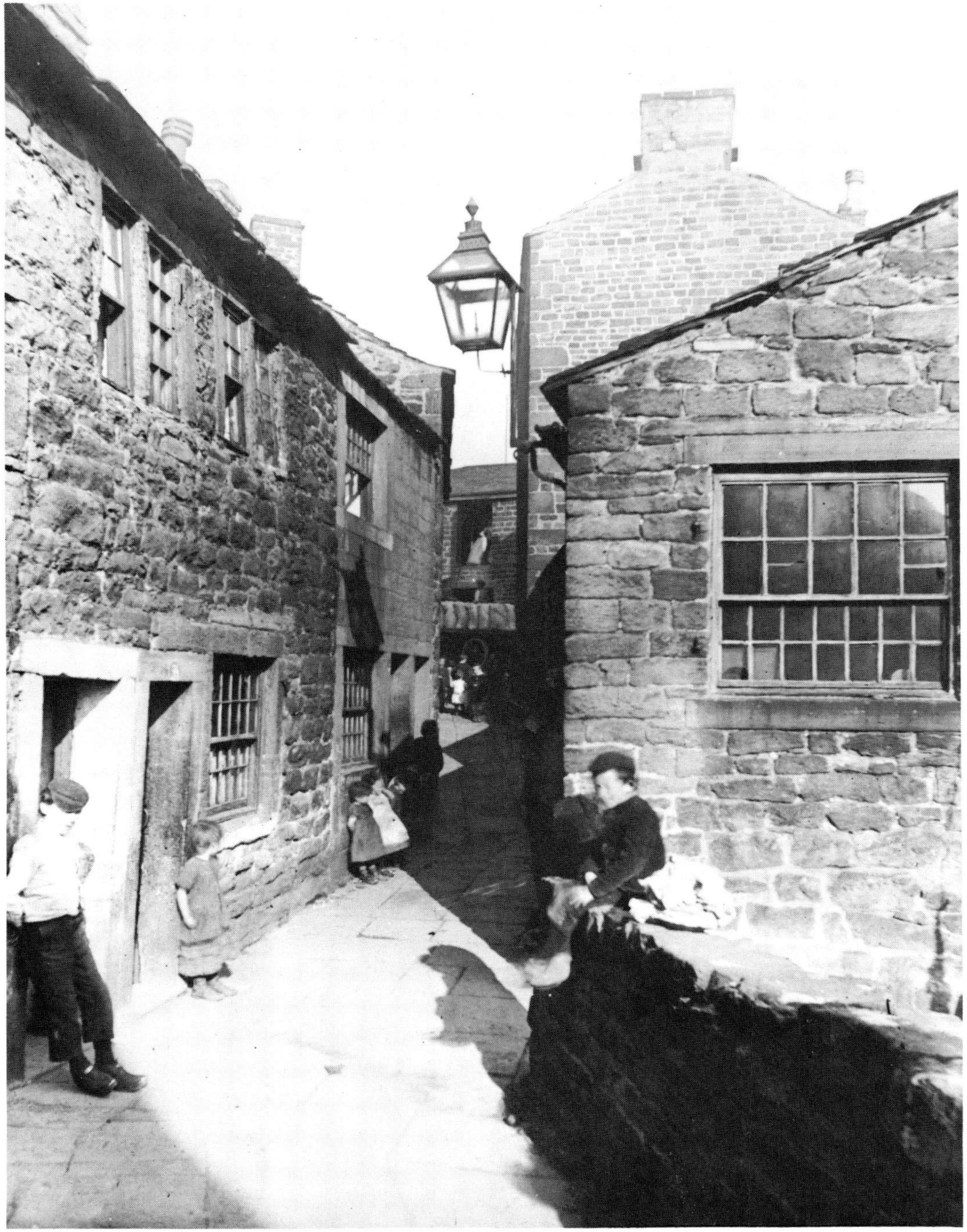

The Ginnel, Westgate, leading to the North Beck, with nineteenth-century slum dwellings.

There was one case of a single privy to twenty-nine houses; another, of three privies to sixty-nine houses. Measles, croup, whooping cough, scarlet fever, enteric fever, typhoid, bronchitis, diphtheria, diarrhoea, erysipelas, consumption . . . all were proving fatal.

A focal point of old Keighley, scene of innumerable "free fights" and "Irish rows"—Quebec Bridge, demolished in 1934 during the Westgate clearance and the covering in of the North Beck.

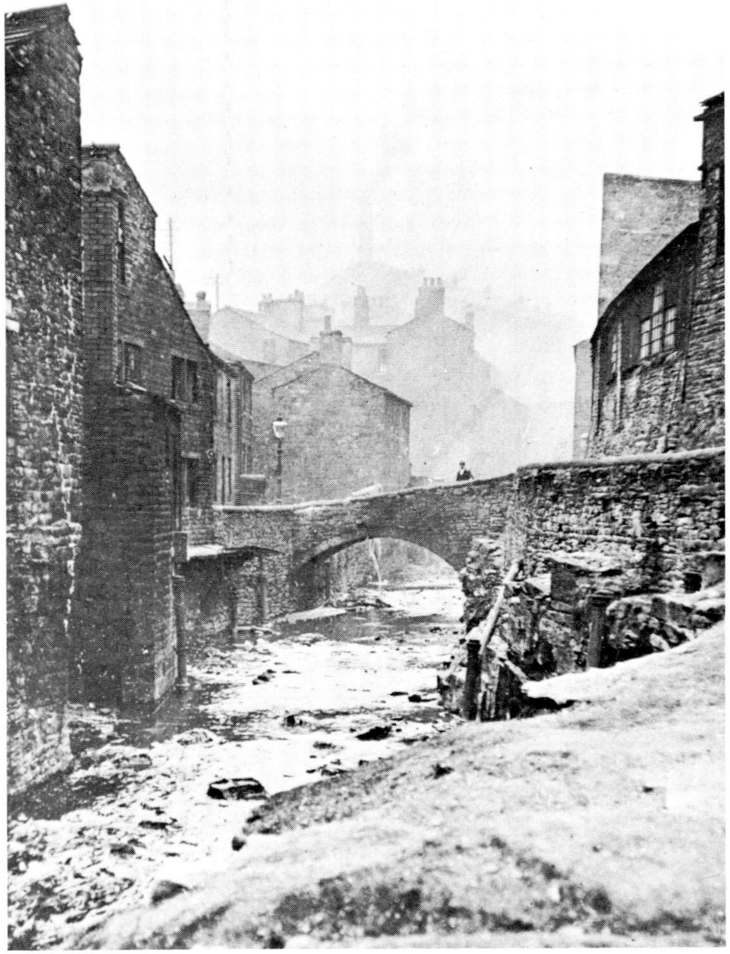

. . . And the view from Quebec Bridge, in 1898.

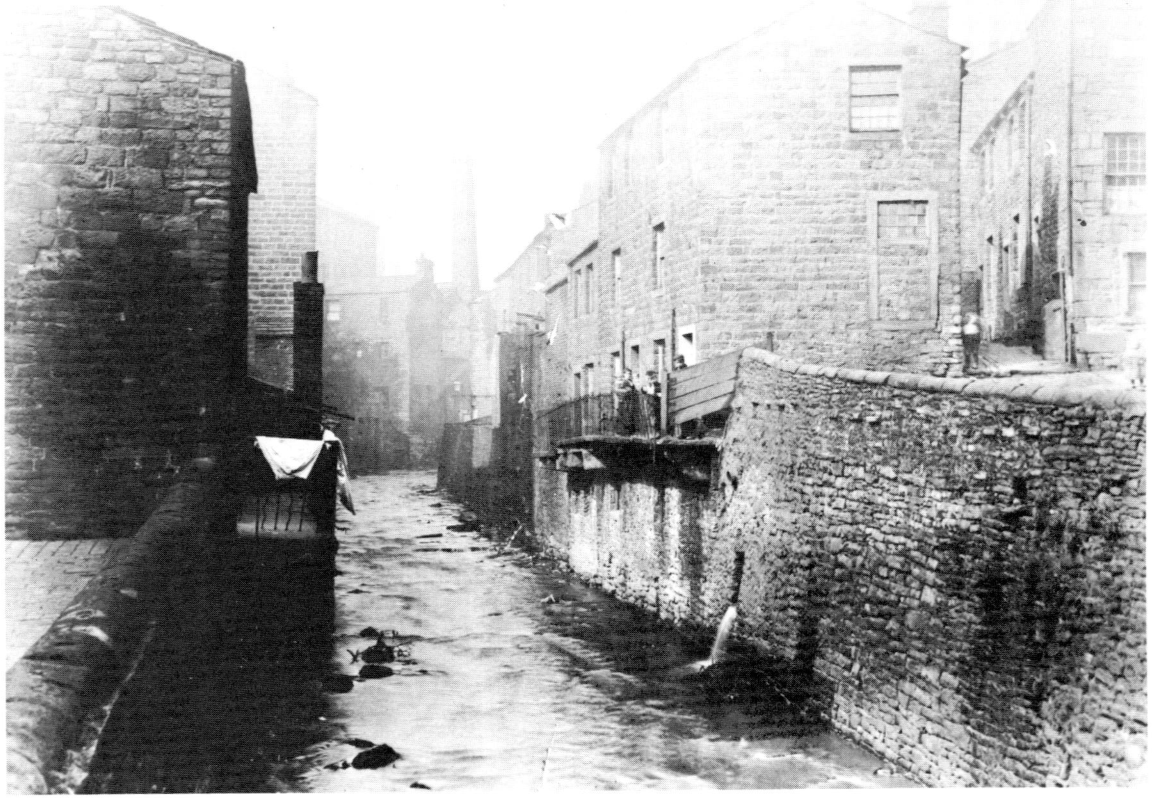

A motley group of Victorian children and adults, squinting into the sun in Westgate. The unhygienic character lounging against the hand-cart is selling hot peas. Of one such tradesman, Sidney "Peacan", persists an unsavoury legend that he stirred his peas up with his wooden leg!

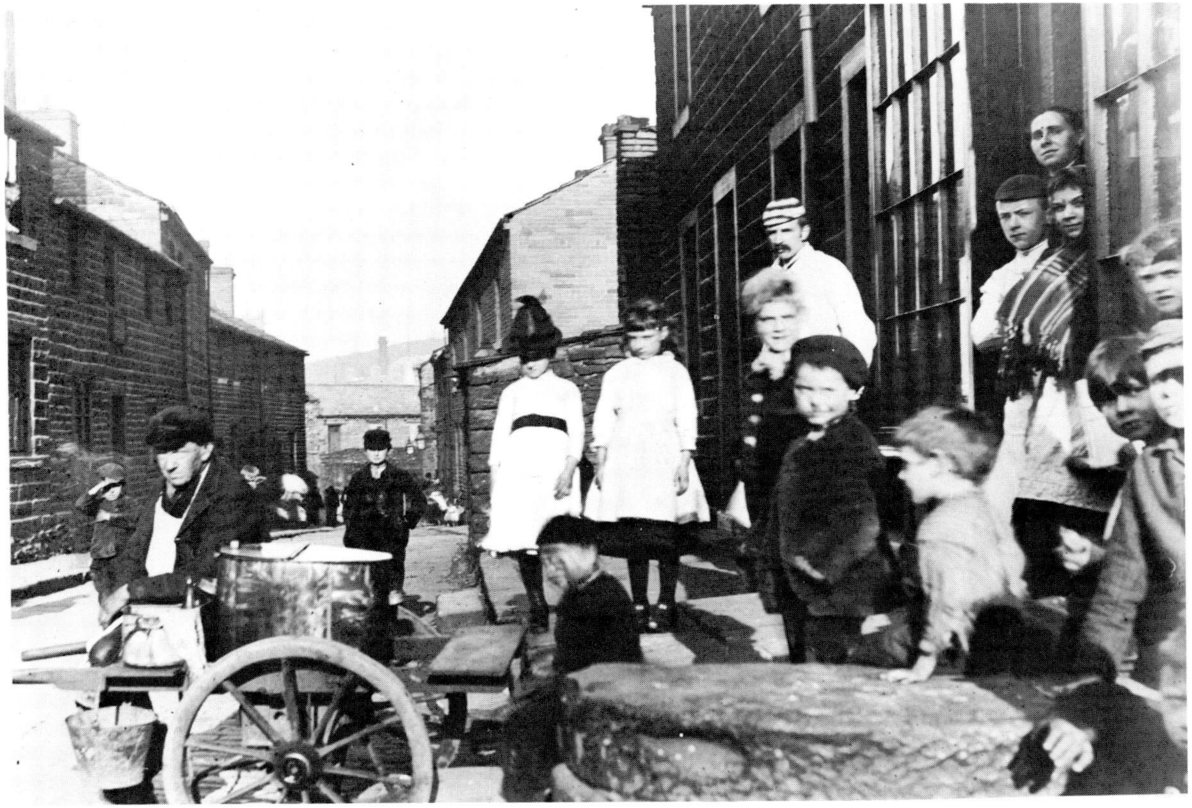

But if conditions were hard, commodities could be relatively cheap. Wadsworth's British and Foreign Fruit and Nut Stores (with assorted staff) in Keighley Market early this century.

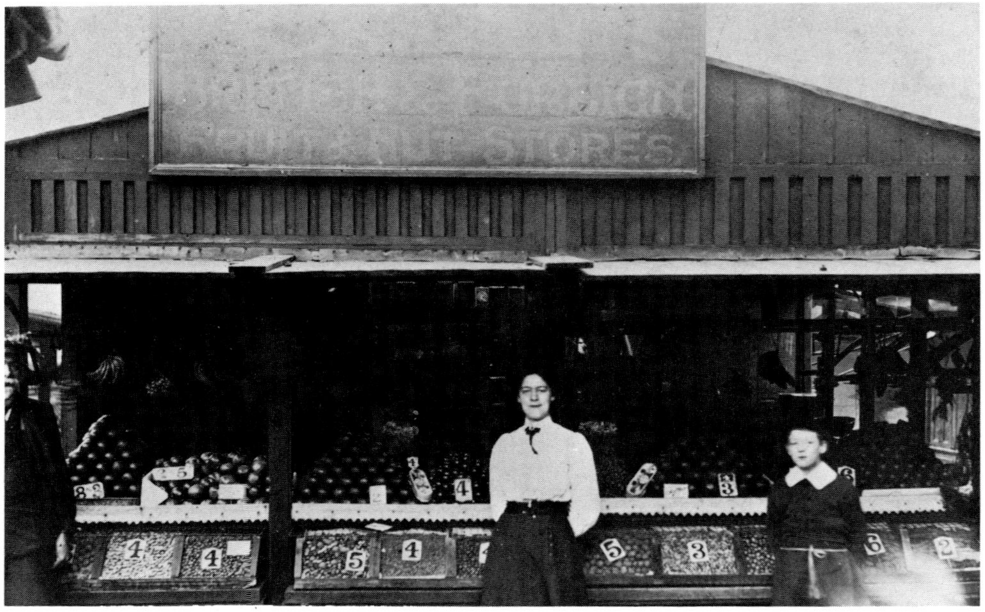

And simple pleasures were near at hand: a roundabout in a fairground which used to occupy spare land at the back of Station Bridge.

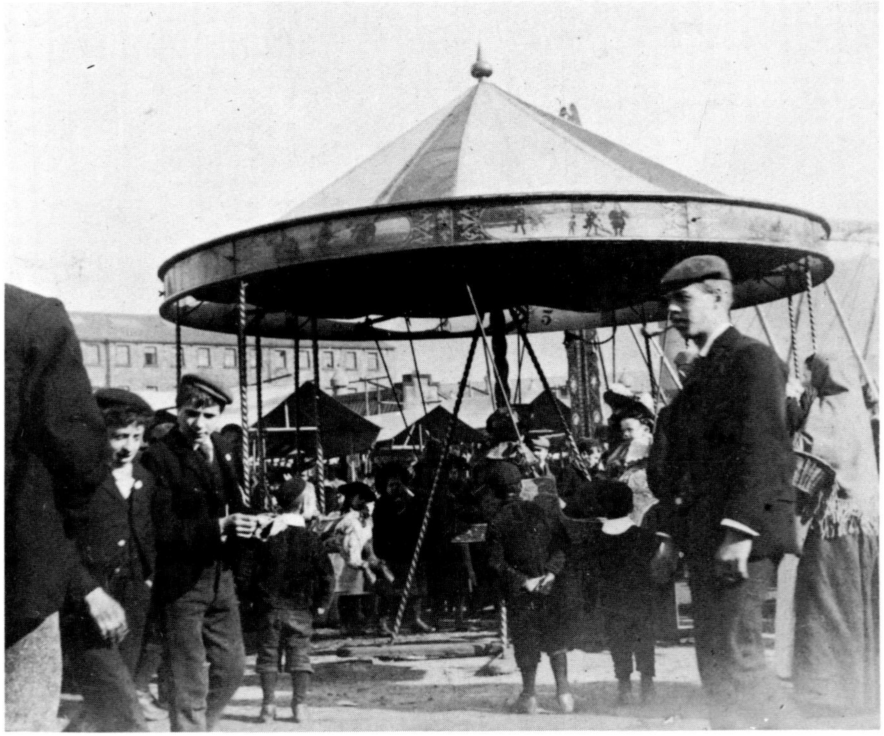

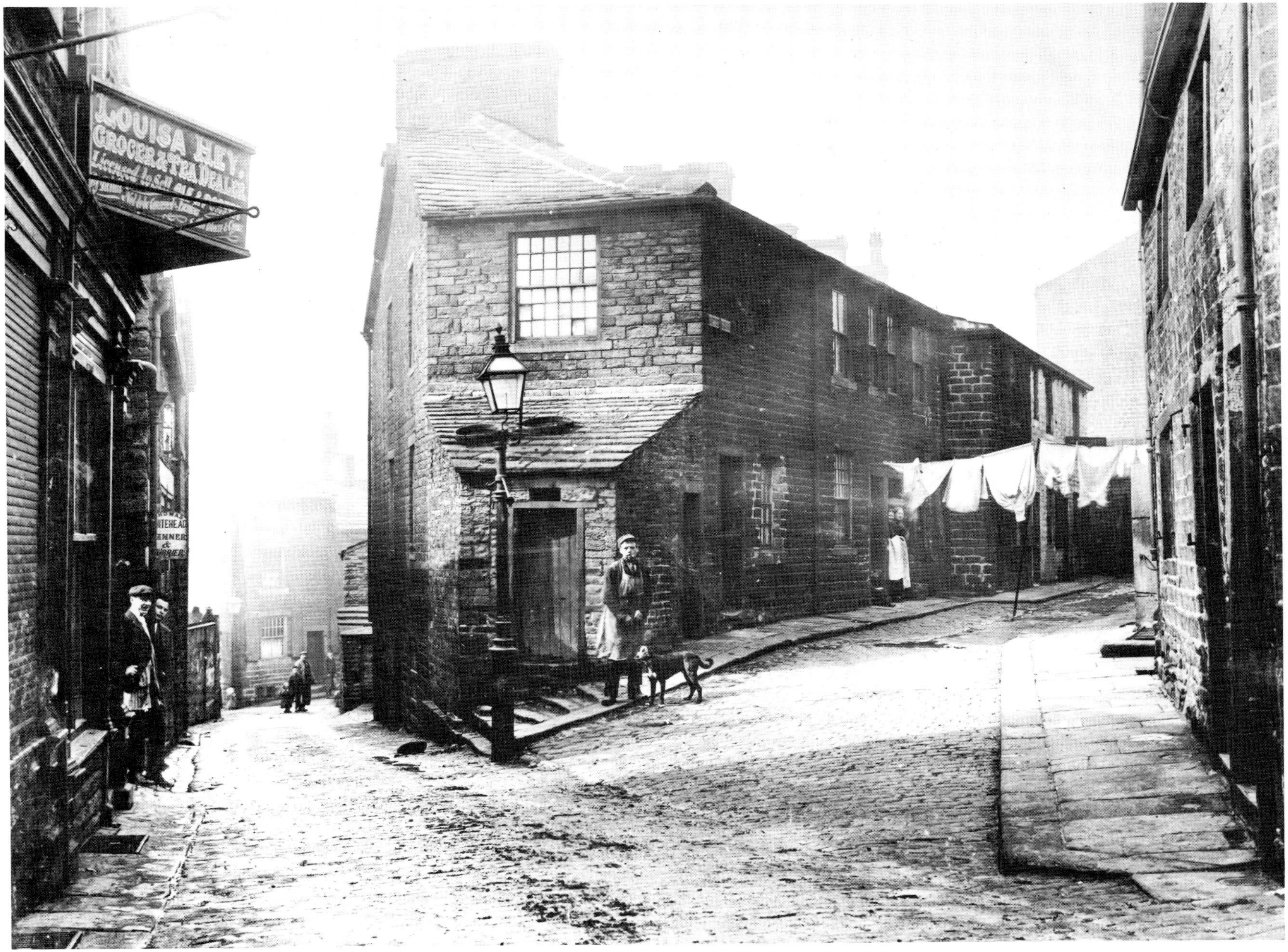

Baptist Square in 1898. Describing this locality in 1853, the Inspector of Nuisances referred to "filthy and offensive premises, from several privies and ash-places, and the ground very uneven, and covered with small cesspools".

Enlarged from the previous photograph, this slaughterman in his stained apron rejoiced in the nickname of "Hiram and Lower'em". There was a rabies scare at the time: in compliance with the regulations, his dog is muzzled.

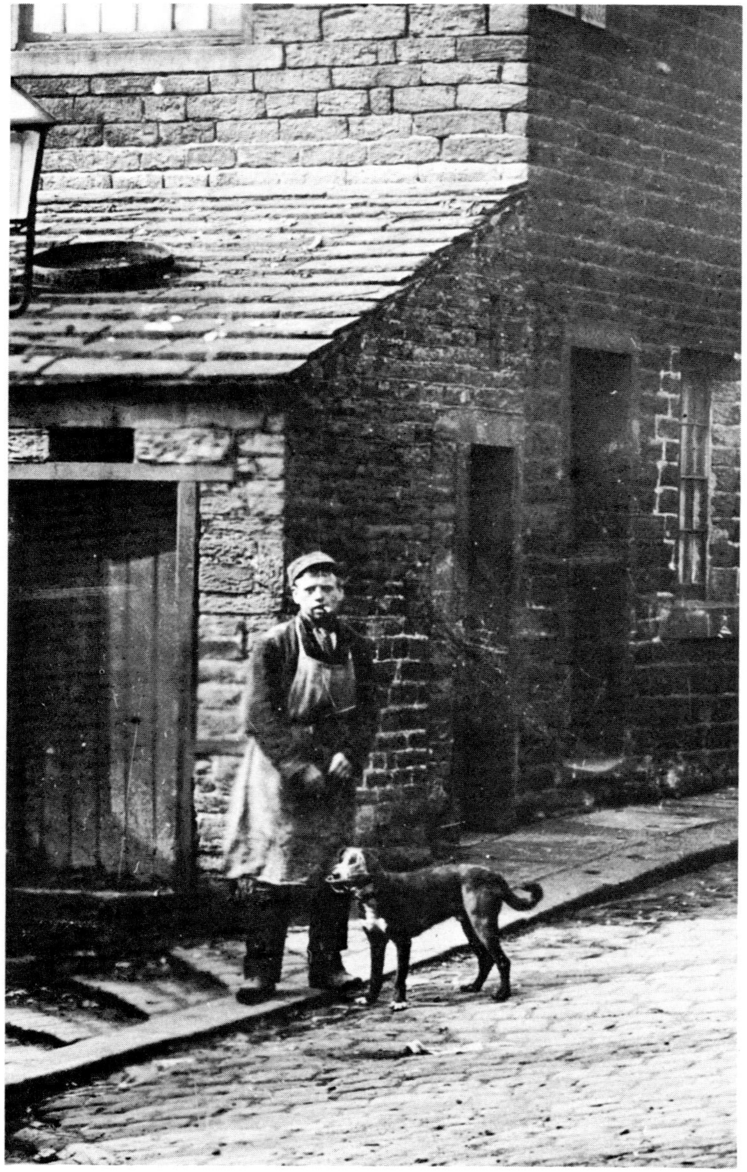

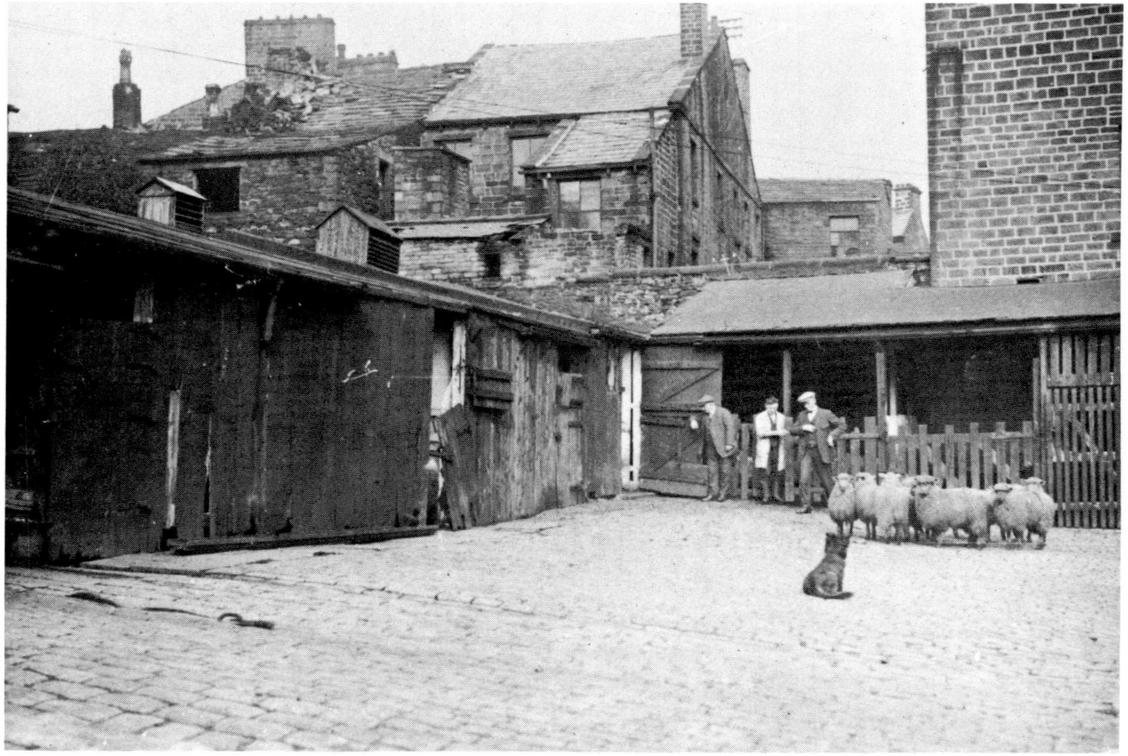

Prior to the opening of the Public Abattoir in 1930, Keighley's slaughtering was carried out in a variety of premises, like this Westgate slaughterhouse, seen with a flock of doomed sheep. This picture tells its own story; though the Medical Officer of Health summed up the situation a few years before its closure—"the Health Committee are fully alive to the inadequacy and unsuitability, from every point of view, of the present accommodation".

The late nineteenth century witnessed the improvement of public amenities. Here, on September 4th, 1888, is the opening of Devonshire Park, on land given by the Duke of Devonshire. The Keighley poet, Bill o' th'Hoylus End, would write quaintly:

"This bonny little garden
  Is fine for perambulators,
Where our handsome servant-lasses
  Can wheel our lovely creatures,
And oh! how happy they will be!
  As time they are beguiling,
When the mammy and the daddy
  Are upon the babies smiling."

This rather dull photograph (it was a showery day) is unusual, for the 1880s, in that the people are unconscious of the camera.

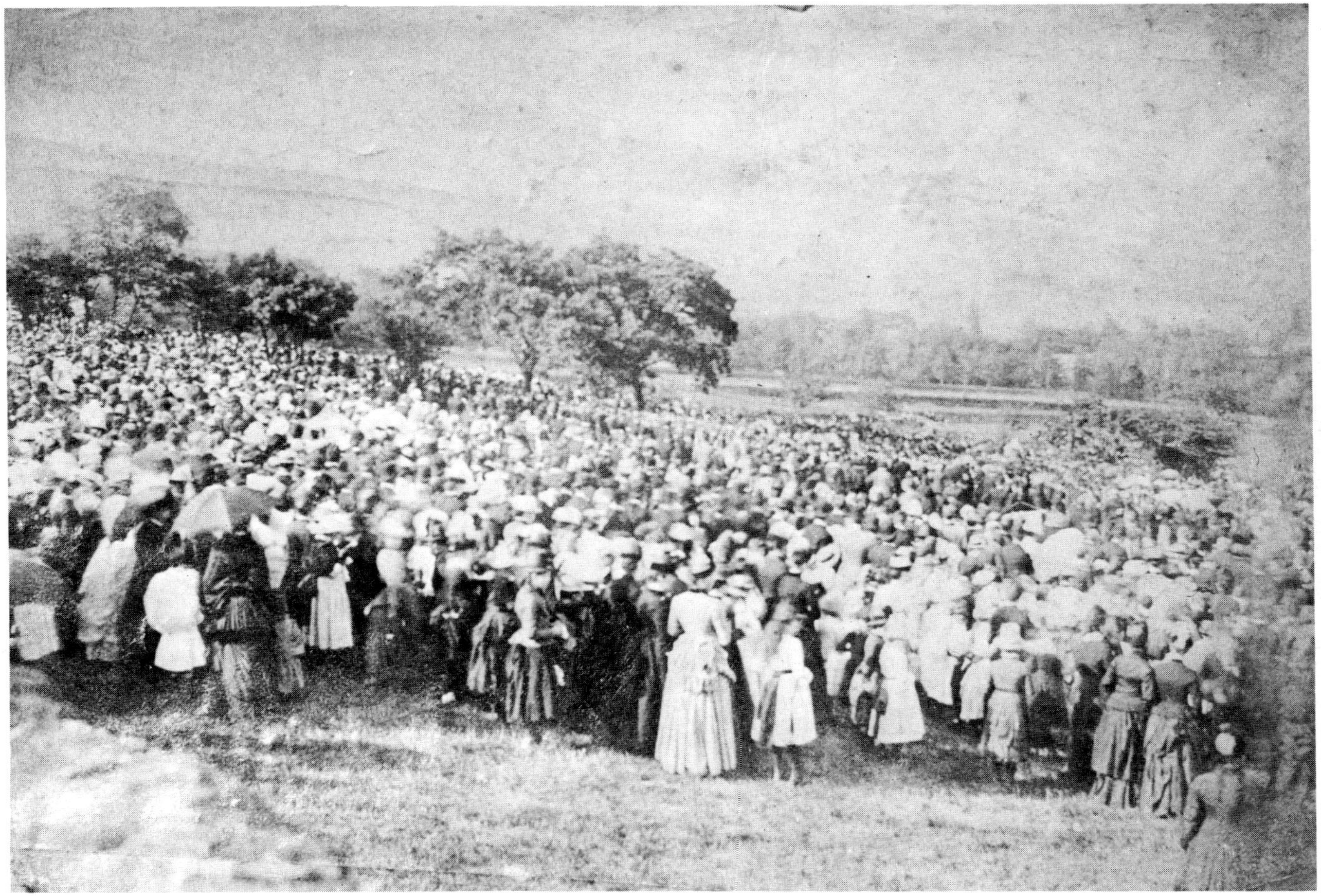

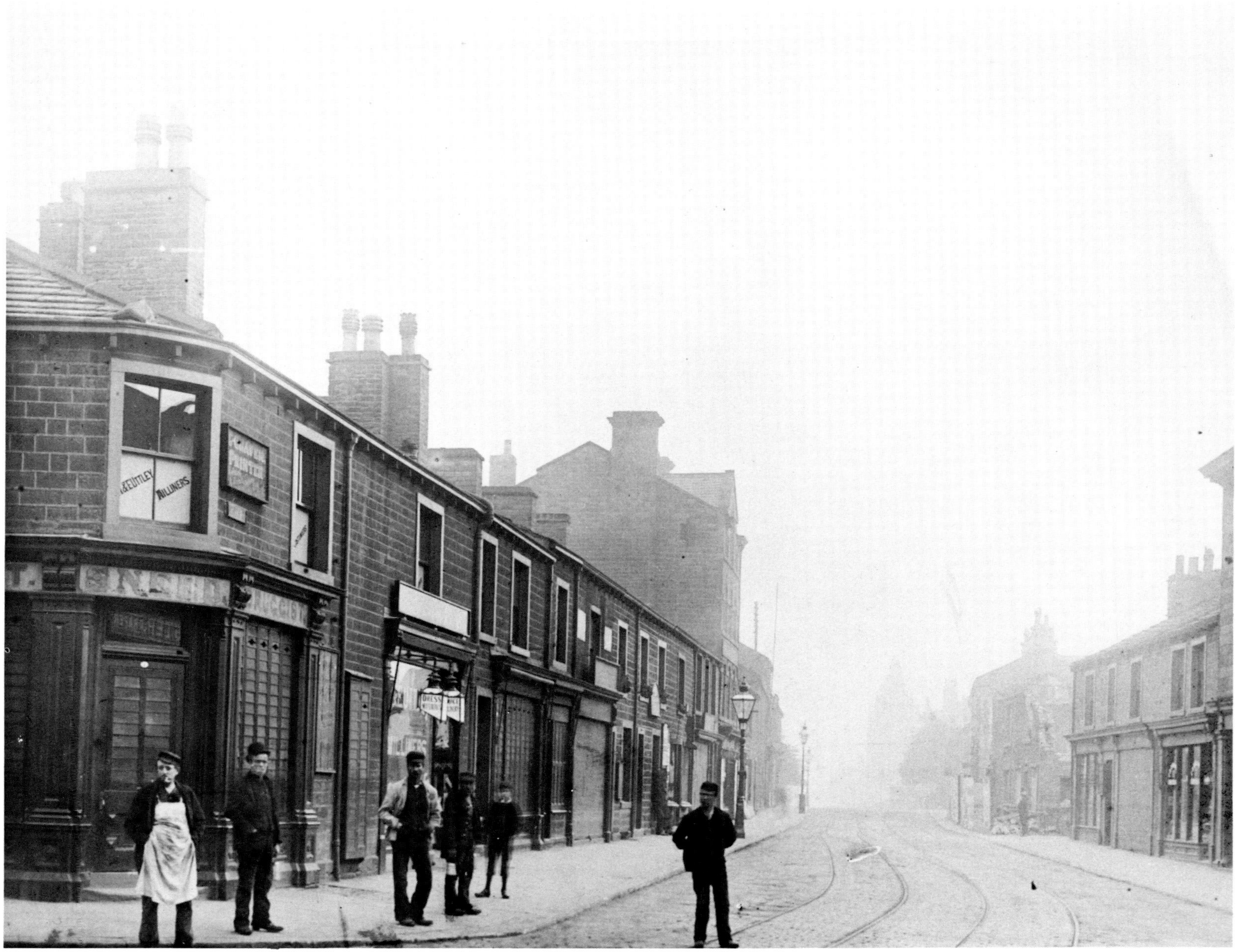

Keighley's main thoroughfare, North Street, viewed from the Cross, or "Sneed's Corner" (after the druggist's shop on the left), about 1890. The road was then only 11 feet wide, as compared with the present 22 feet. The rails, for horse-trams, had been laid in 1889. Demolition is in progress on the right-hand side.

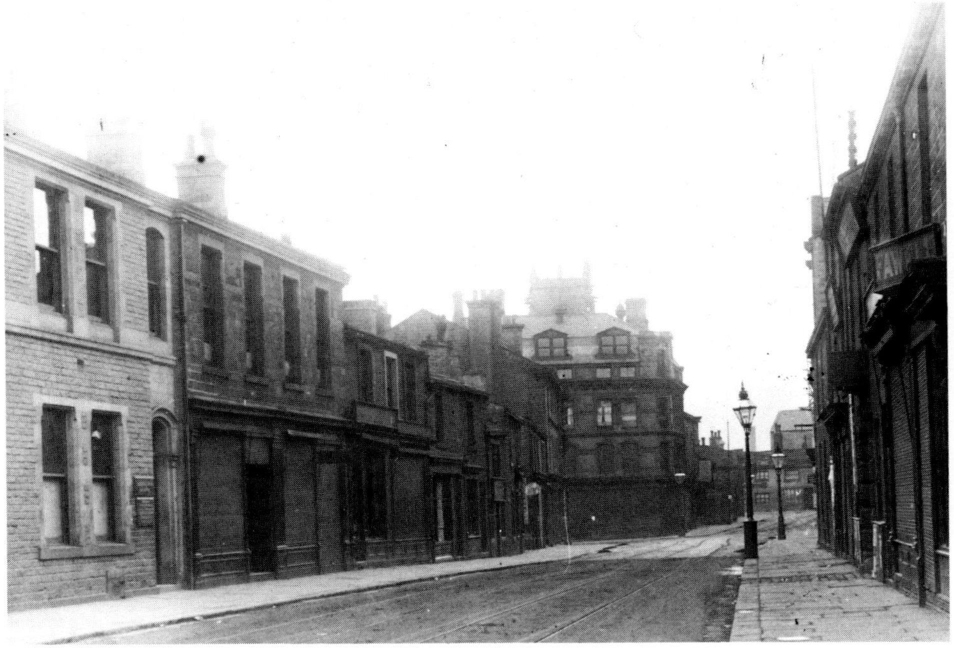

And, seen from the opposite direction, late Victorian shutters and an empty Church Green.

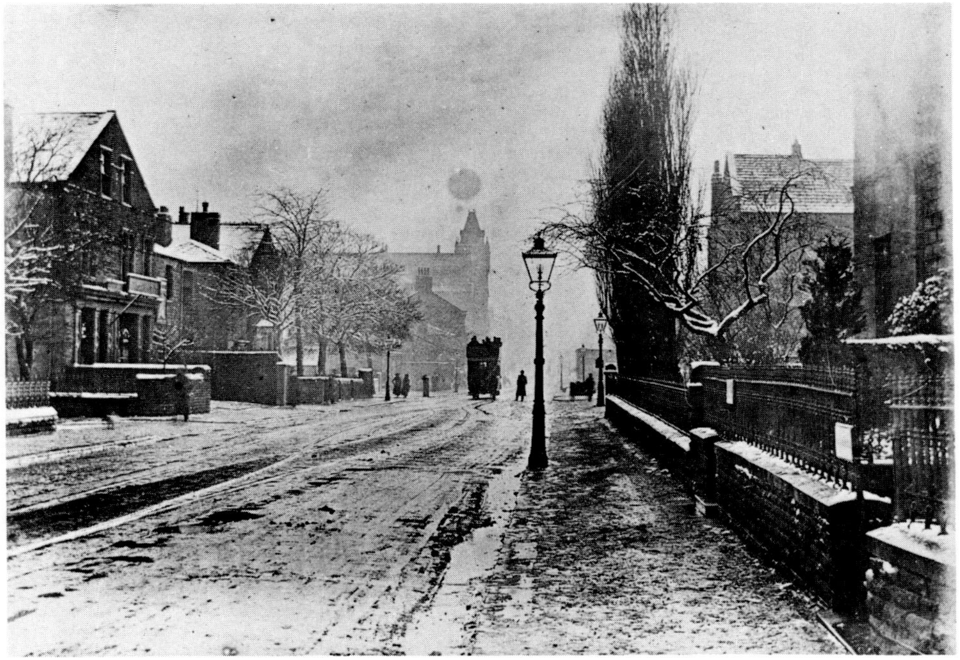

Winter scene in Skipton Road before the advent of the internal combustion engine.

North Street and the Keighley Mechanics' Institute, its tower still minus the clock presented by Prince Smith in 1892. Houses with gardens still occupy the left-hand side, wooden shops the right.

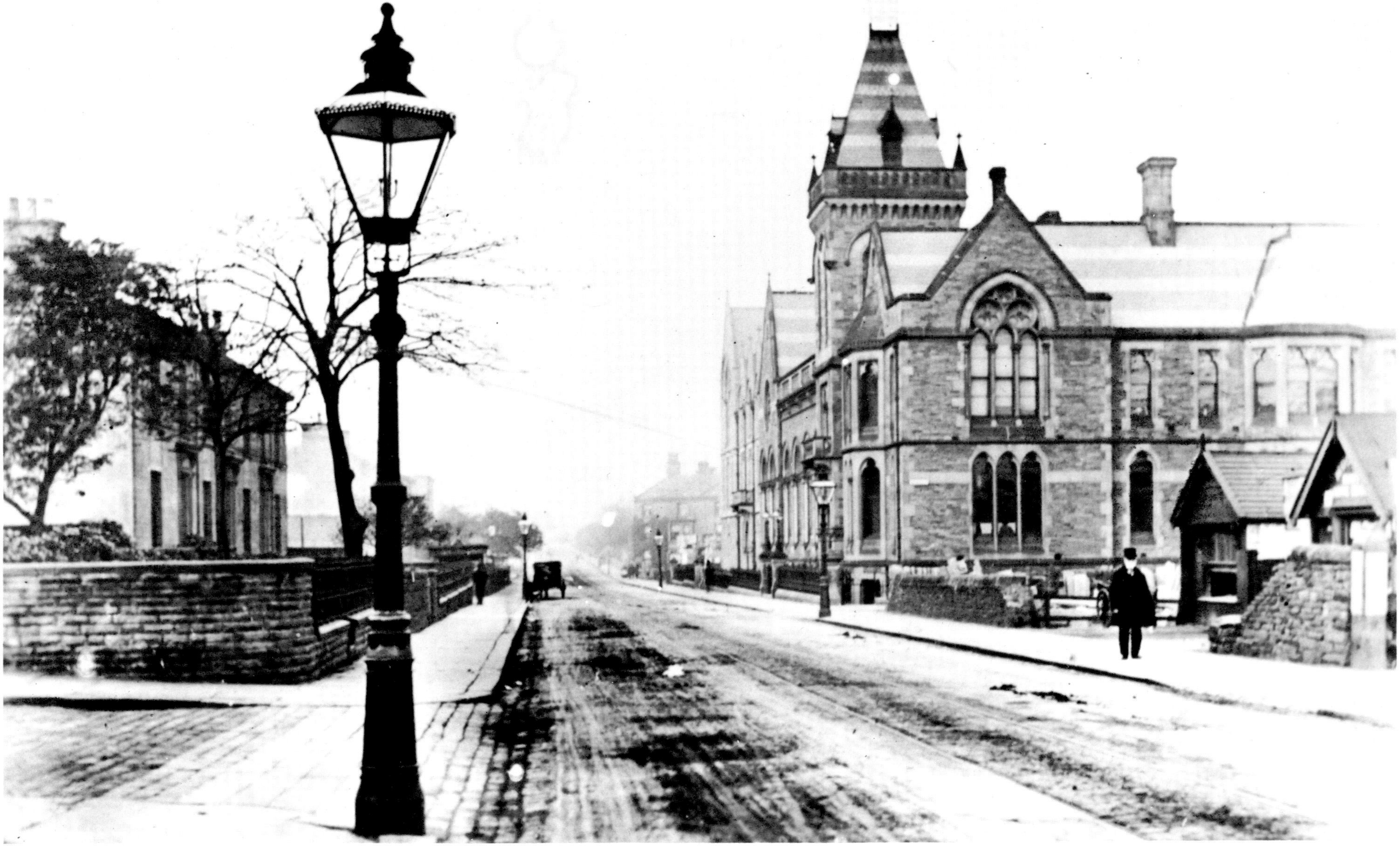

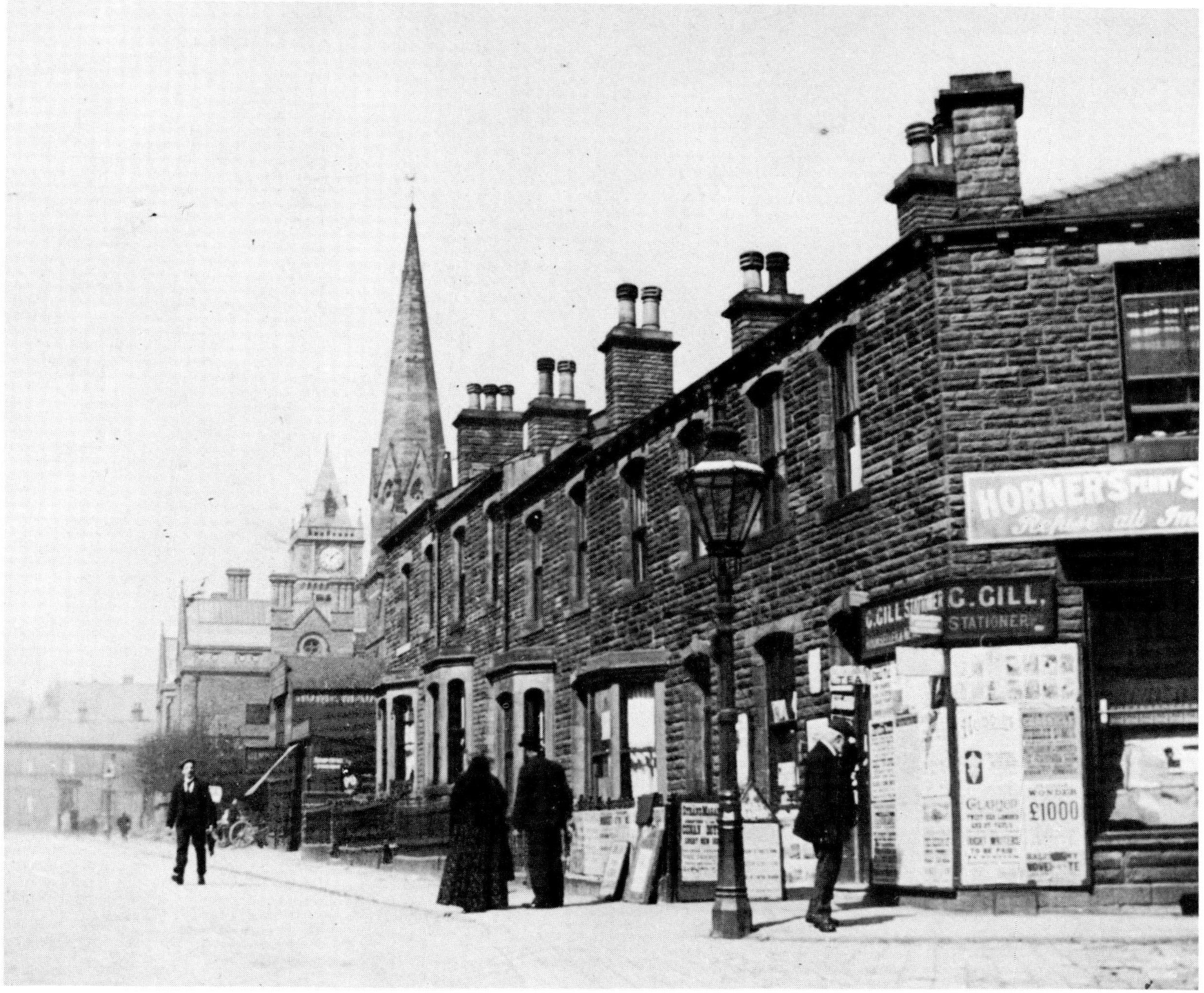

Cavendish Street. A poster outside C. Gill's stationer's mentions the 1897 Jubilee. There are wooden buildings at the end of Henry Street; and, beyond, the United Methodist Free Church, popularly called the "Cock Chapel" in honour of its weathercock, the highest in Keighley. Crowing 125 feet above the street, this was a landmark for nearly seventy years. At the top of Cavendish Street stands North Terrace, site of the future Public Library.

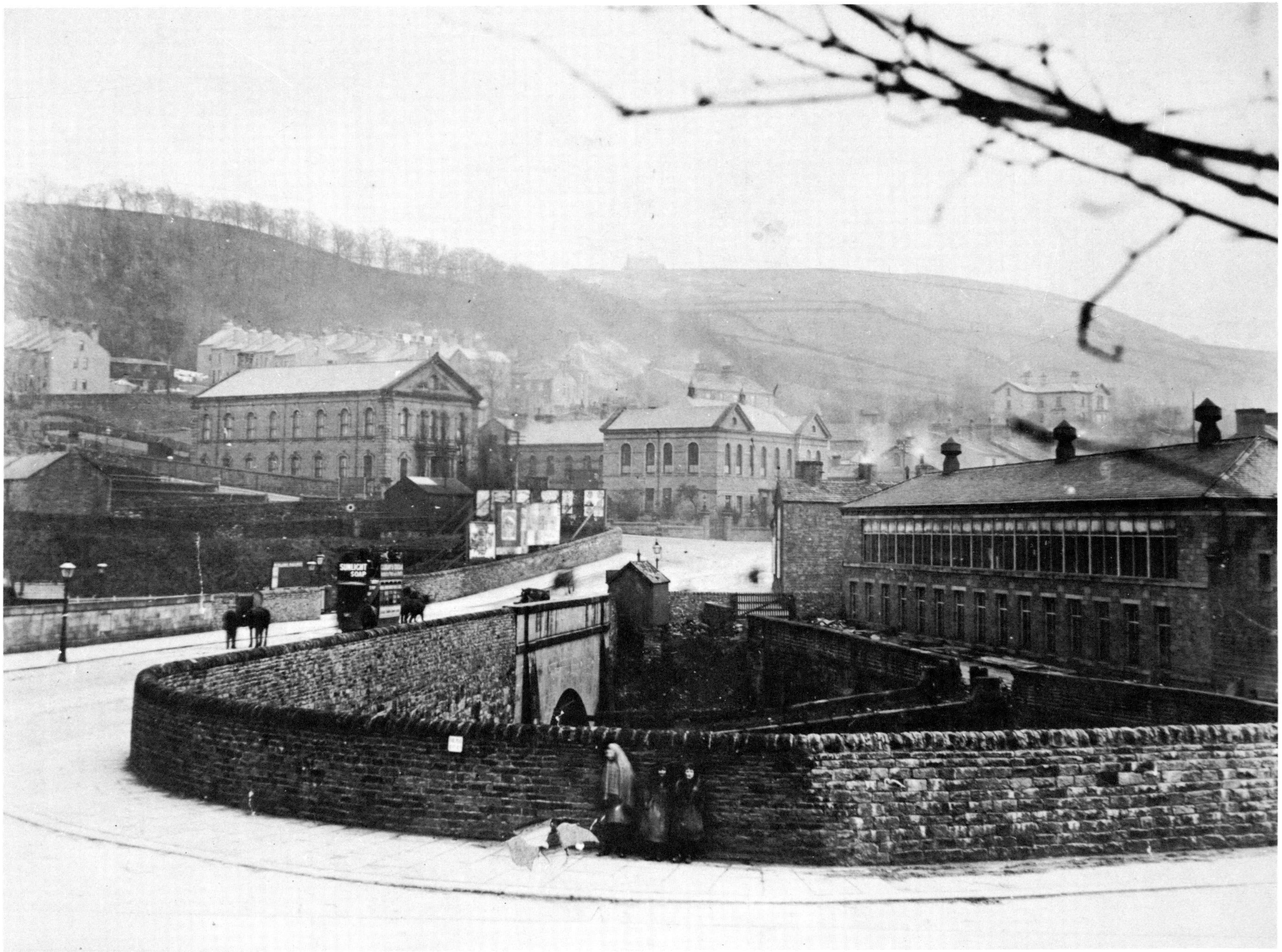

Ingrow Bridge in 1898. A horse-bus, advertising the inevitable Sunlight Soap, makes its leisurely way up to Wesley Place.

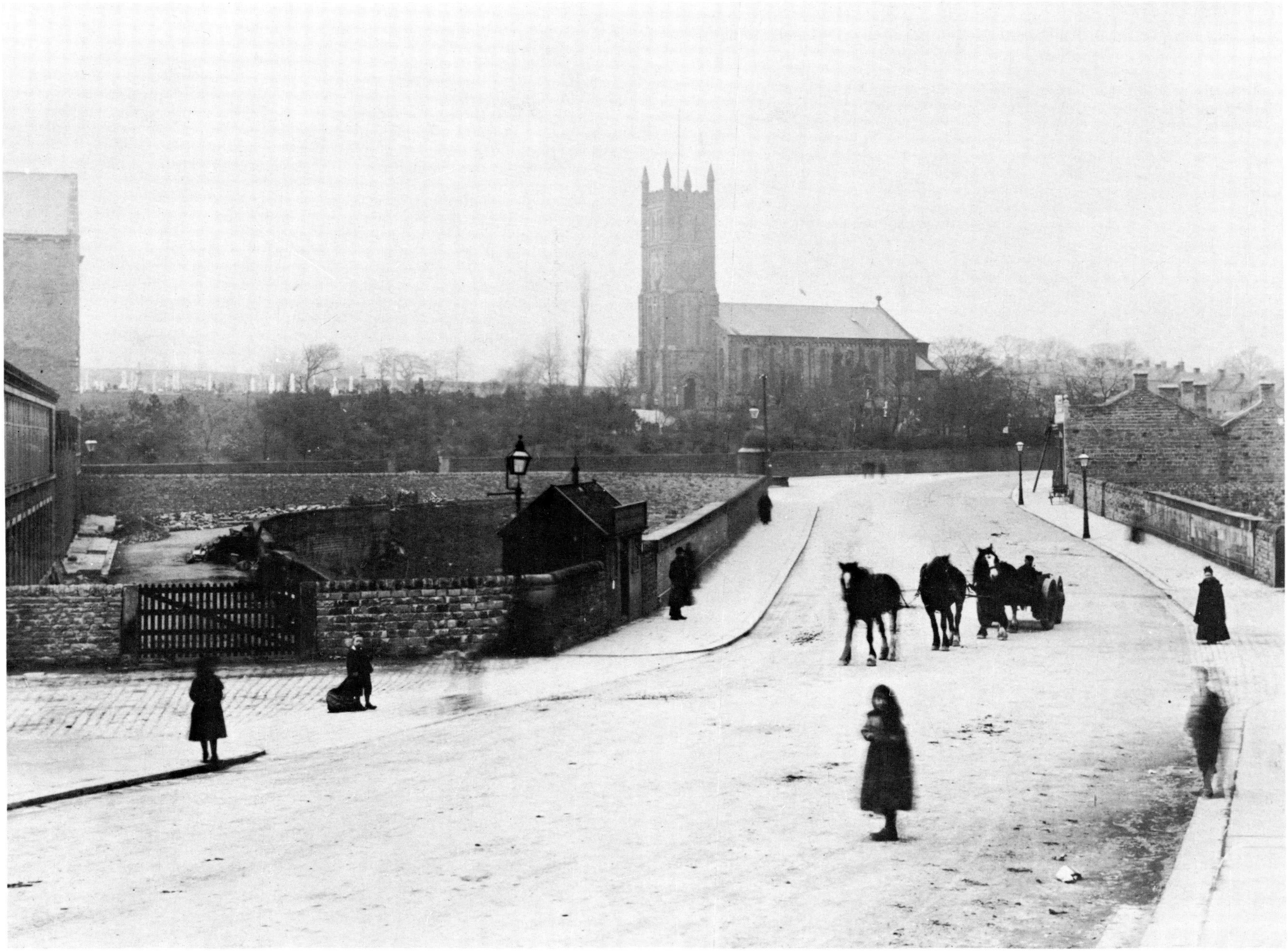

. . . And the view back from Wesley Place towards Ingrow St. John's Church, built "in the Norman style" and consecrated in 1843.

Turn-of-the-century traffic-jam: a carriage, a cab and a horse-bus confront one another at the Cross.

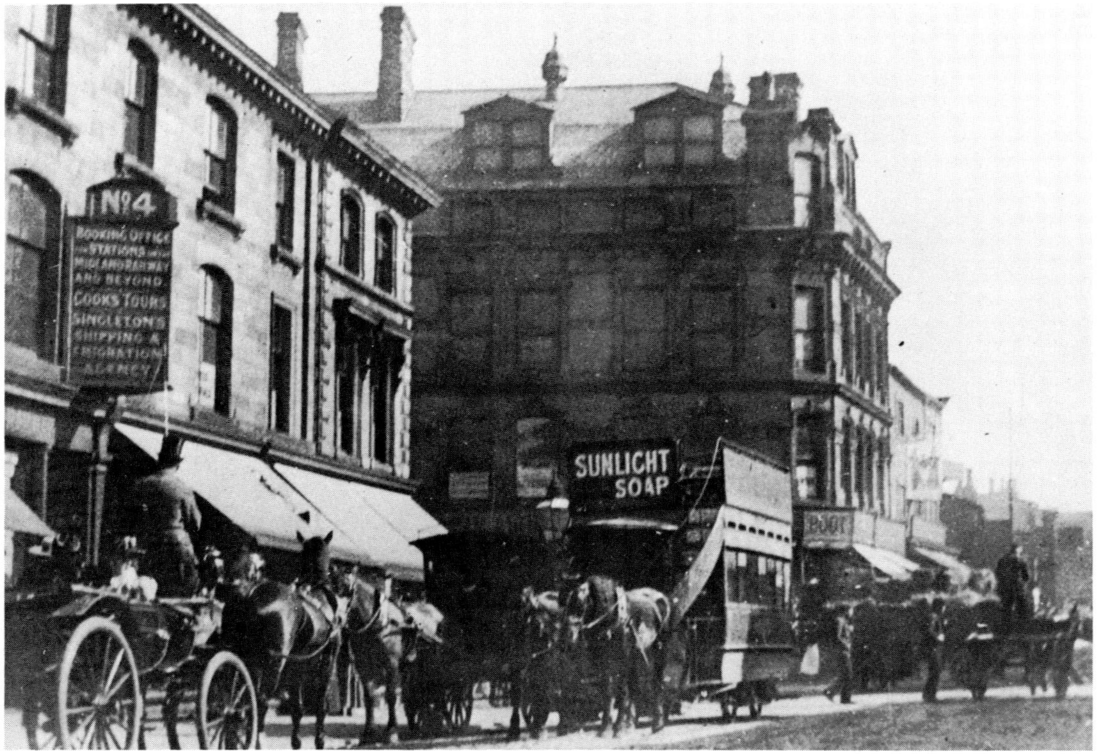

And Low Street, perpetually busy.

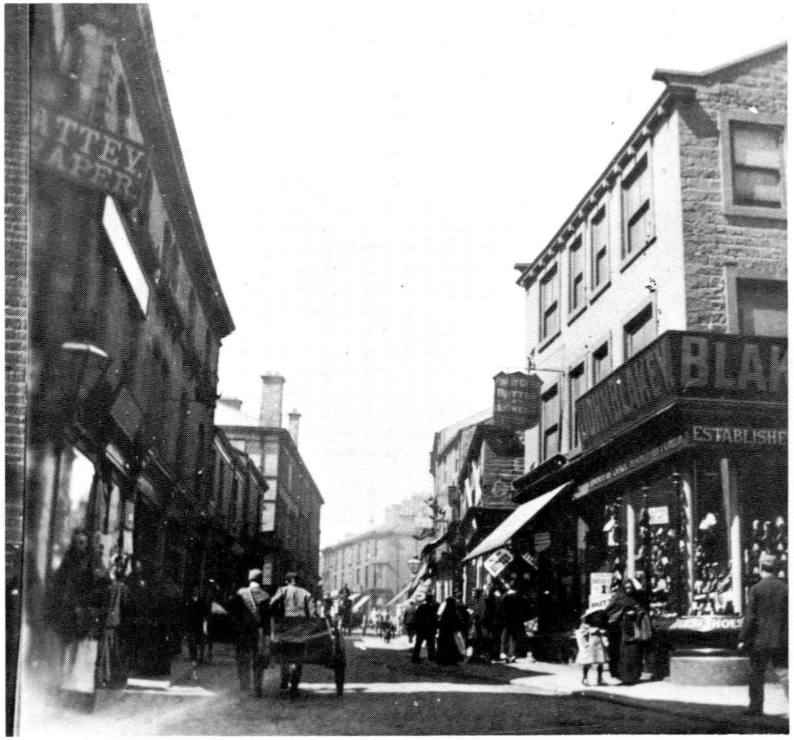

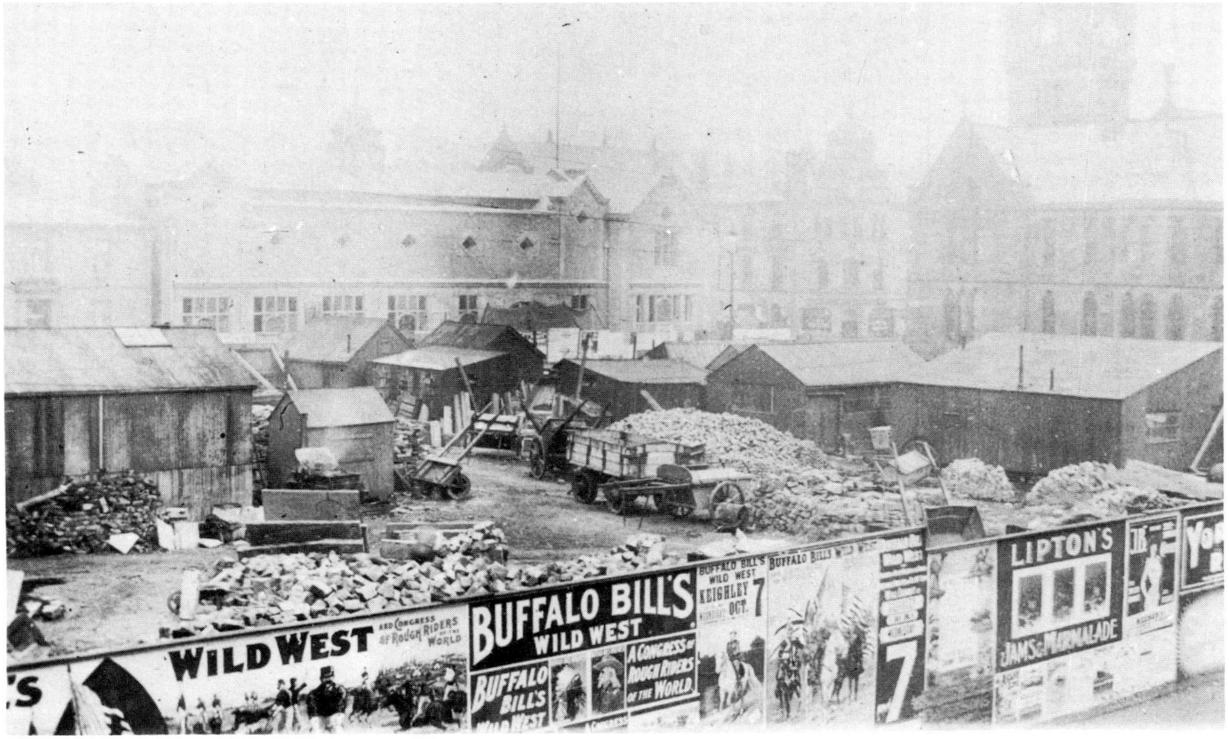

The Corporation stone-yard, later the site of the Town Hall Square, with wooden premises on the North Street-Cavendish Street corner. This photograph was taken in the autumn of 1903—the hoardings are advertising the visit of Buffalo Bill's Wild West show on October 7th. Beyond, on the right, the Mechanics' Institute; whilst to the left, England's first Carnegie Library is not quite finished.

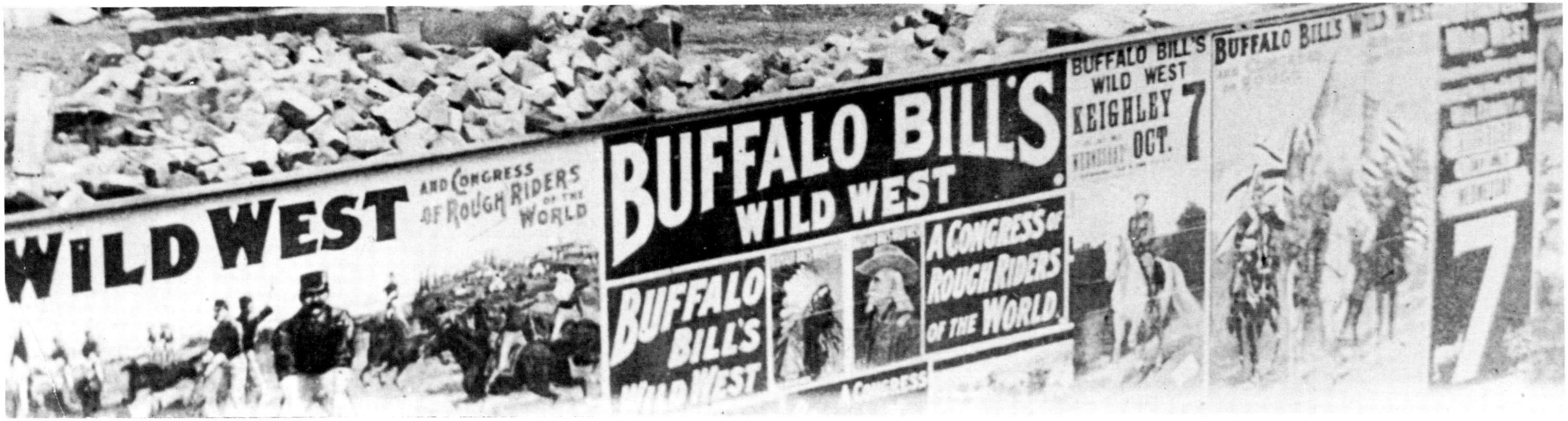

Keighley's horse and cattle fairs, traditionally held in May and November, were the occasion for general holidays and entertainments. These cows stand for sale in Russell Street, about 1905, when increased traffic had already pushed business off the main thoroughfares. Afterwards, the fire brigade would hose the streets.

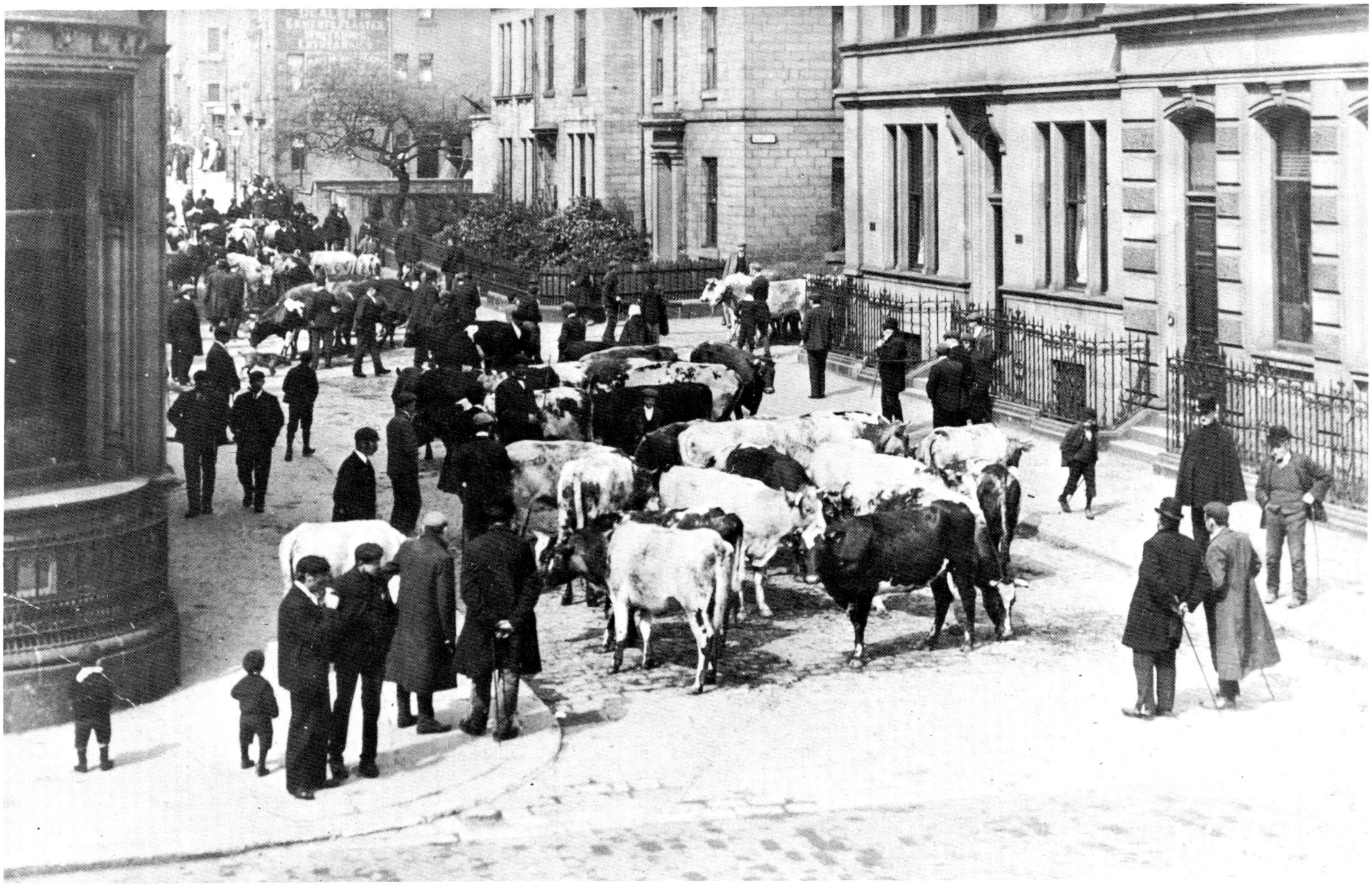

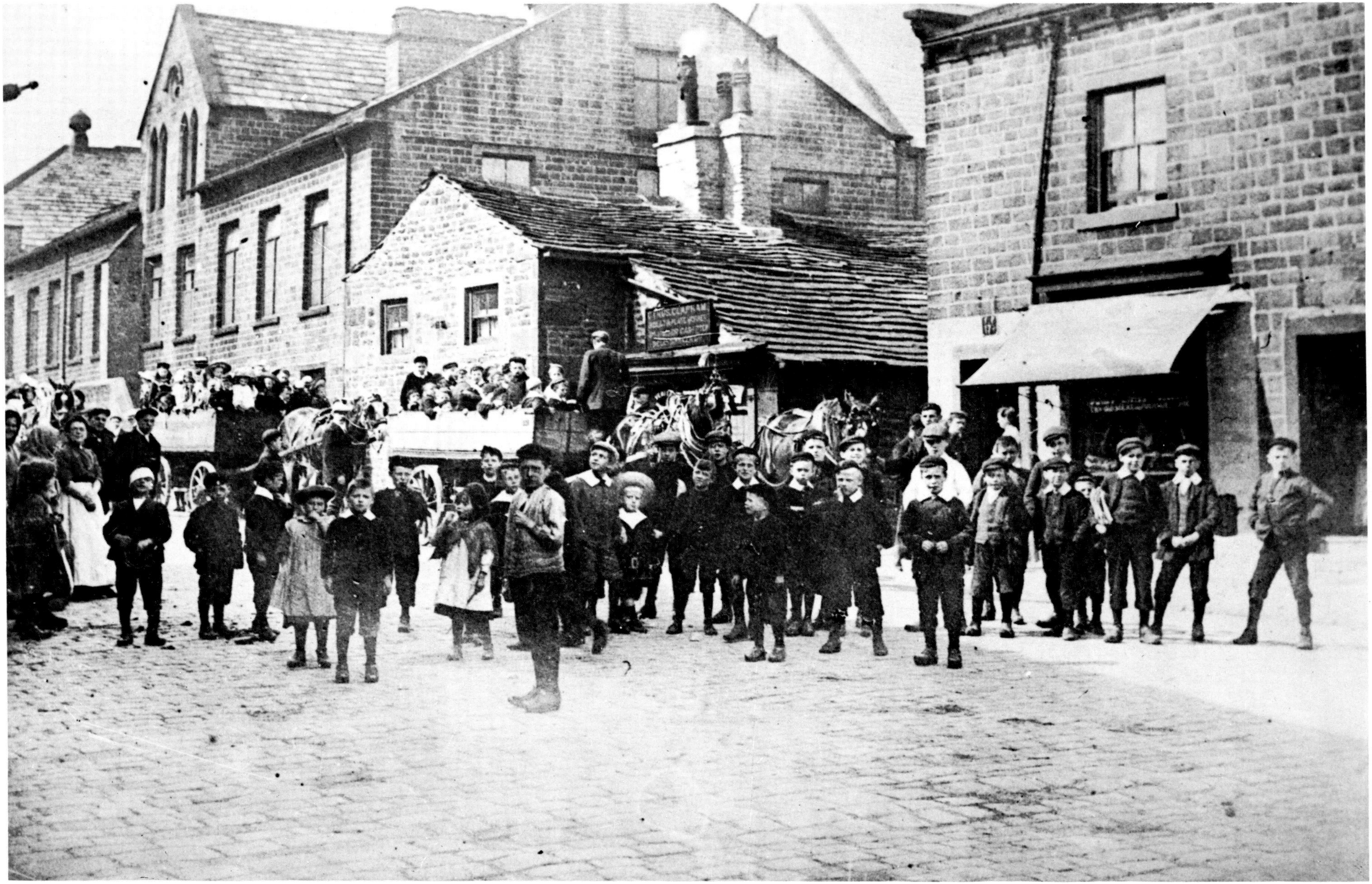

Edwardian children: the start of a Sunday School outing in carts, from the bottom of West Lane. The premises of Cyrus Clapham, tin-plate worker, occupy the present National School playground. Suresnes Road has replaced the shop on the right.

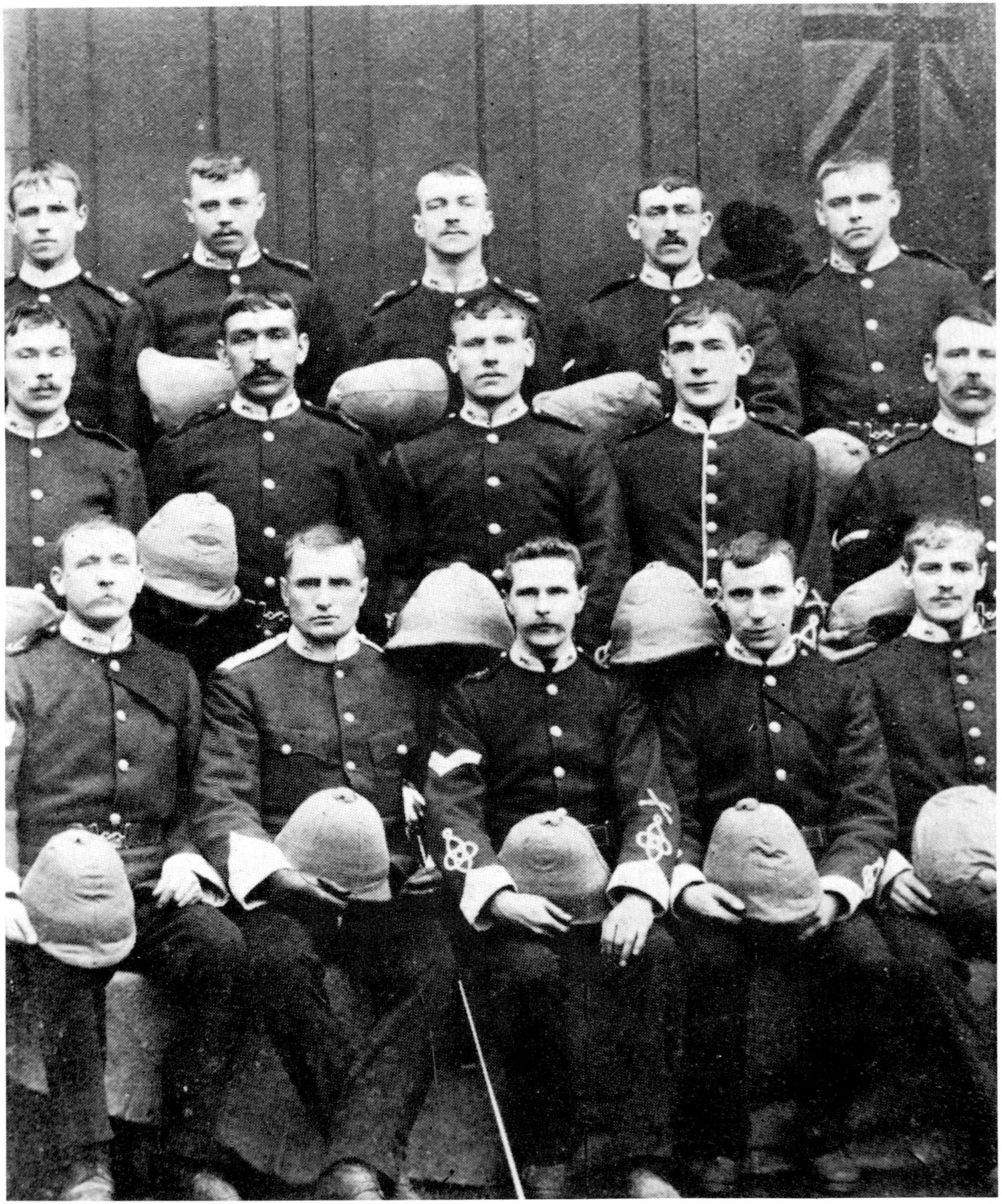

Military tradition waxed strong in Keighley. At the turn of the century, local companies of the 3rd Volunteer Battalion Duke of Wellington's (West Riding) Regiment mustered a total strength of 313, from which was formed an Active Service Contingent for the South African War (1899-1902). These men were photographed outside the Drill Hall on January 23rd, 1900, prior to their departure for regimental headquarters at Halifax. "The streets were densely thronged with people," records one contemporary account, "the mills and workshops having ceased work at noon in order to enable the workpeople to join in the send-off".

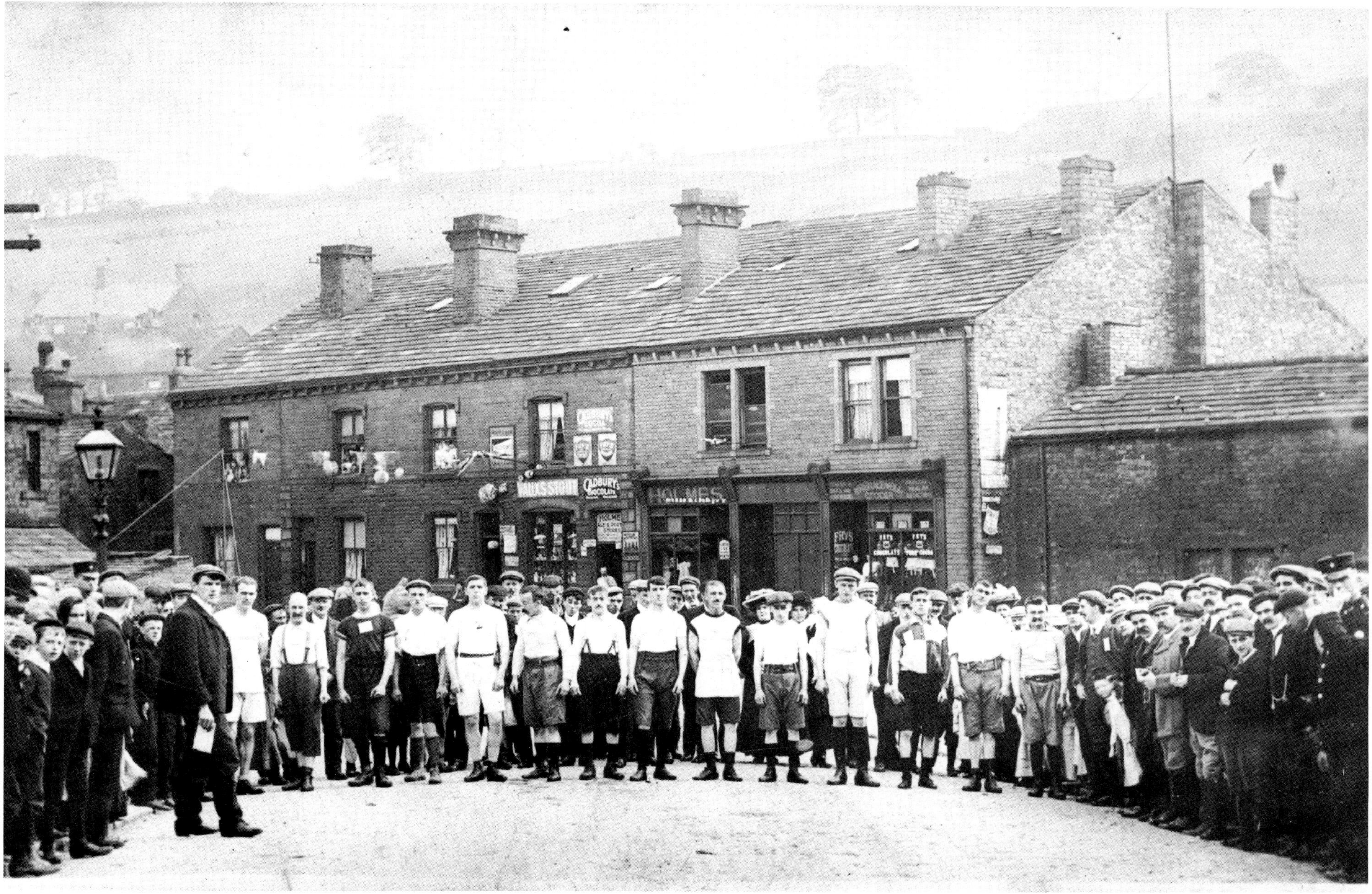

Leisure was often spent actively. Walking matches were the craze in the early years of the century: the starting line-up at a Worth Village Gala.

Athletic clubs were popular seventy years ago. The Lees and Cross Roads Institute Gymnastic Team forming pyramids in the street. The meagre crowd, glimpsed between their upturned heads and arms, does not appear unduly impressed.

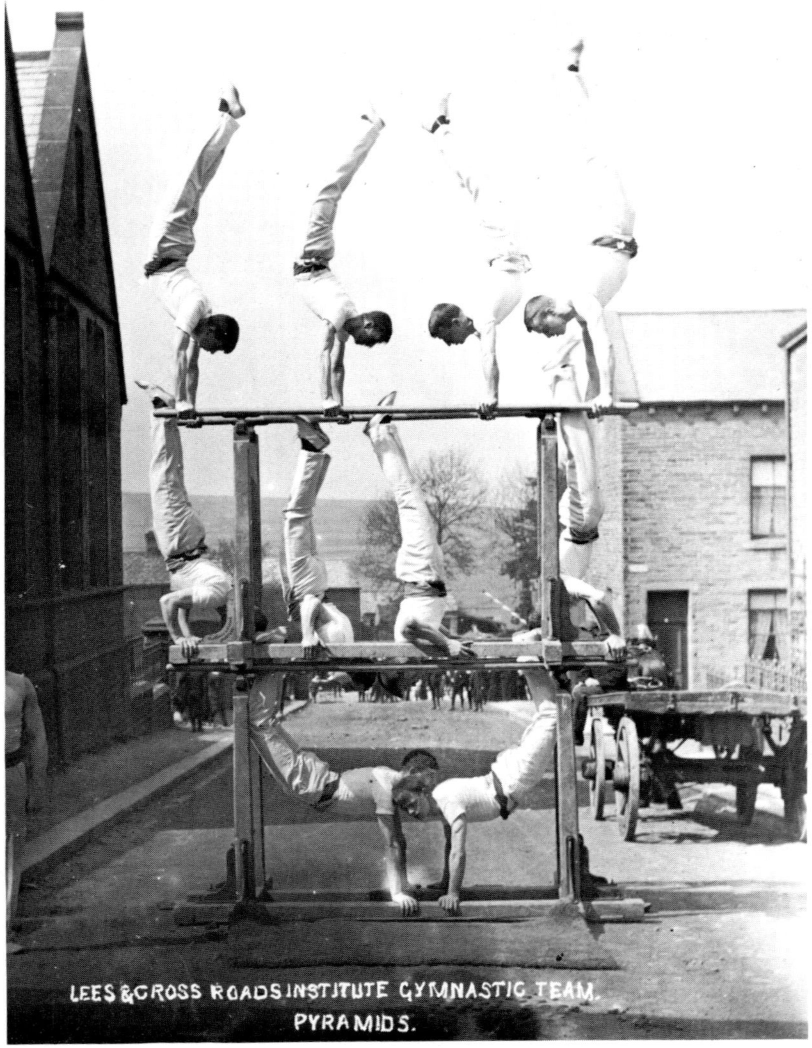

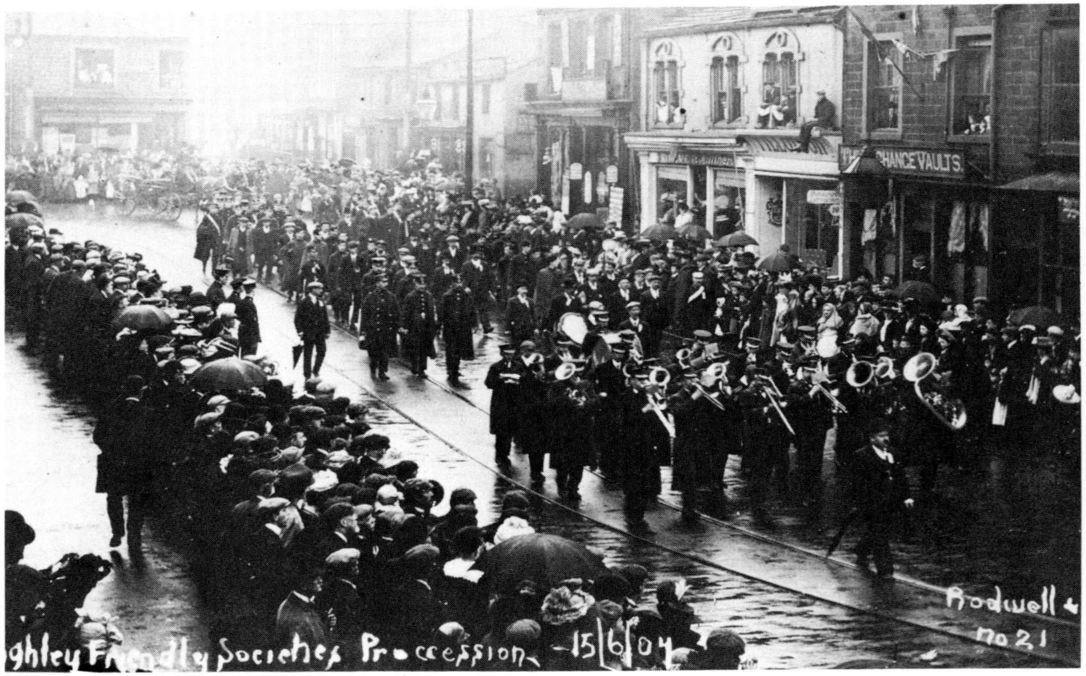

Kildwick Brass Band marches stolidly through the rain down Keighley High Street, during the Friendly Societies' Gala of 1907. Some of the shops have changed little since. Next to the Exchange Vaults, bold lads from Tillotson's Paperhangers sit outside the upstairs windows.

The Edwardians loved a good procession, and the coronation of Edward VII in 1902 launched a spectacular series of historical tableaux through Keighley streets. Here, scholars from St. Barnabas's Sunday School, Thwaites Brow, depict "Pope Gregory and Saxon Children".

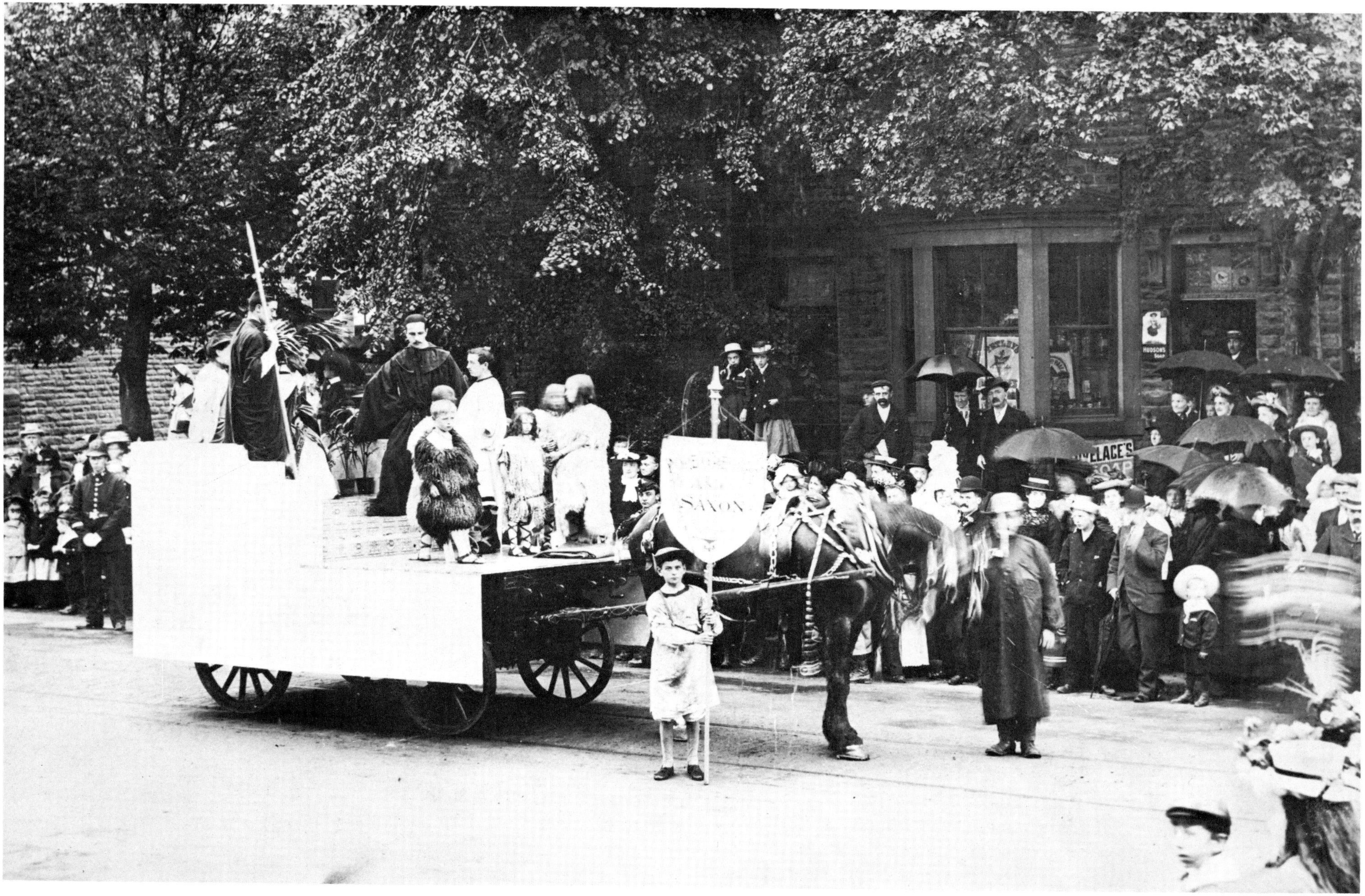

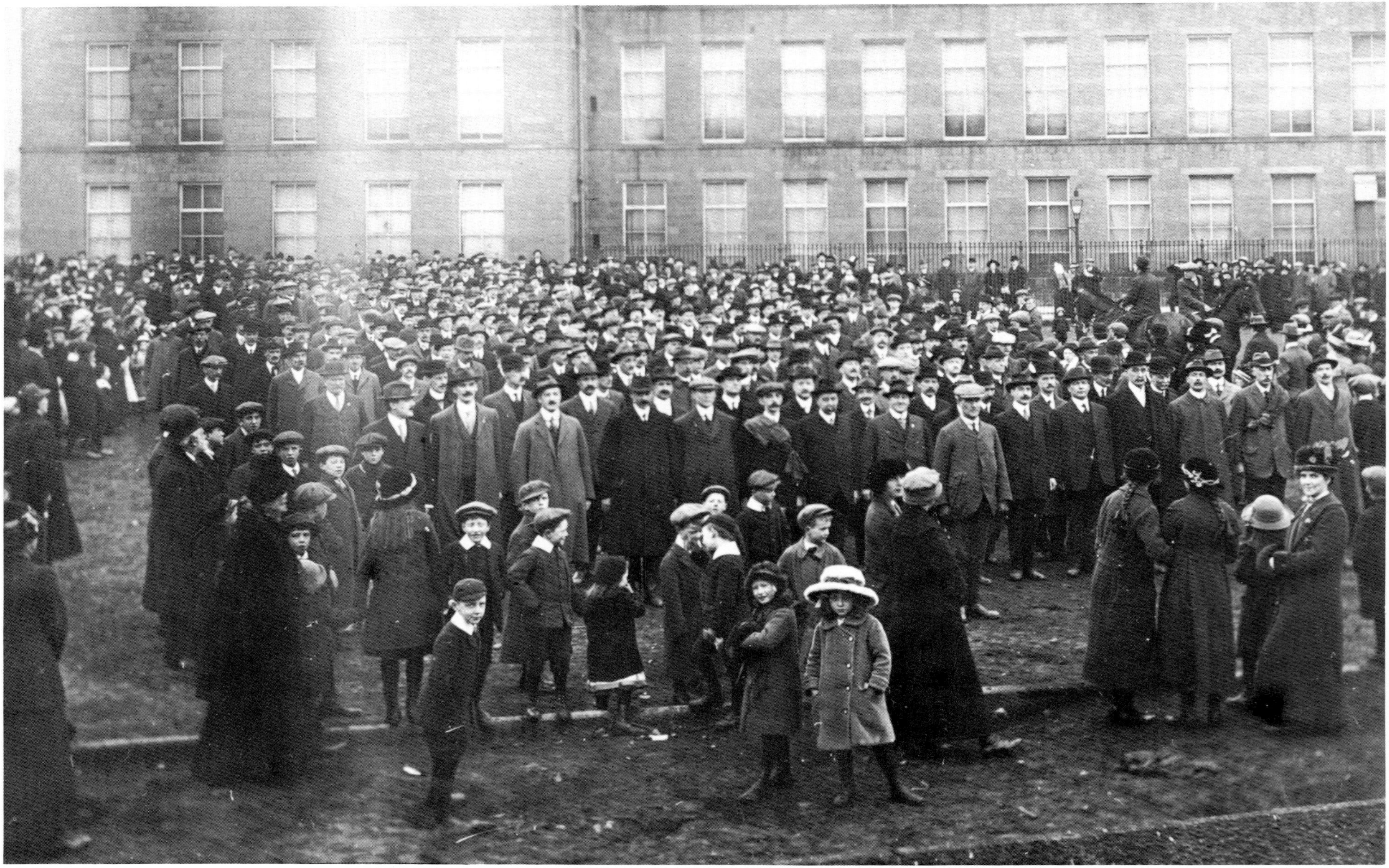

The Great War shattered the stability of generations, and life would never be the same again. Dignified gentlemen of the Keighley Civil Volunteers parading at Sutton Mill in March, 1915. Their commander is Mr. Leolin Brigg. Two possibly old campaigners in the front rank are carrying their rolled raincoats slung over the shoulder. Notice, too, the small mounted contingent, more ornamental than useful.

The Keighley coat-of-arms, formed from the combined shields and crests of the Keighley and Cavendish families, seen here with an additional inscription "To the Brave Sons of Holy Russia". This sycamore panel, designed by T. C. Butterfield, headmaster at the Keighley School of Art, and and carved by Private Anthony Boothman of the West Yorkshire Regiment, was dispatched for the Anglo-Russian Hospital, Petrograd, early in 1917. Overtaken by the Revolution, it disappeared.

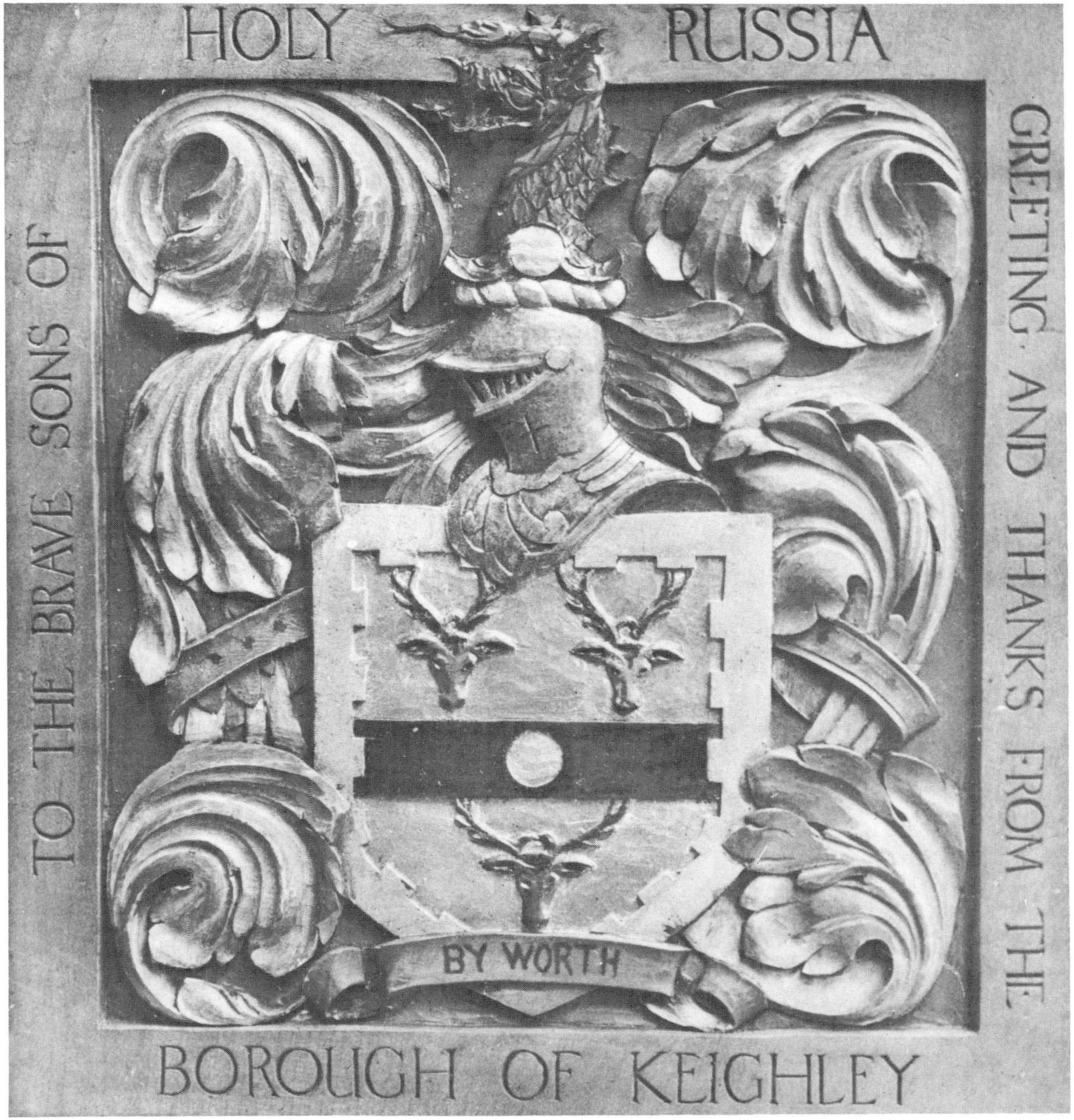

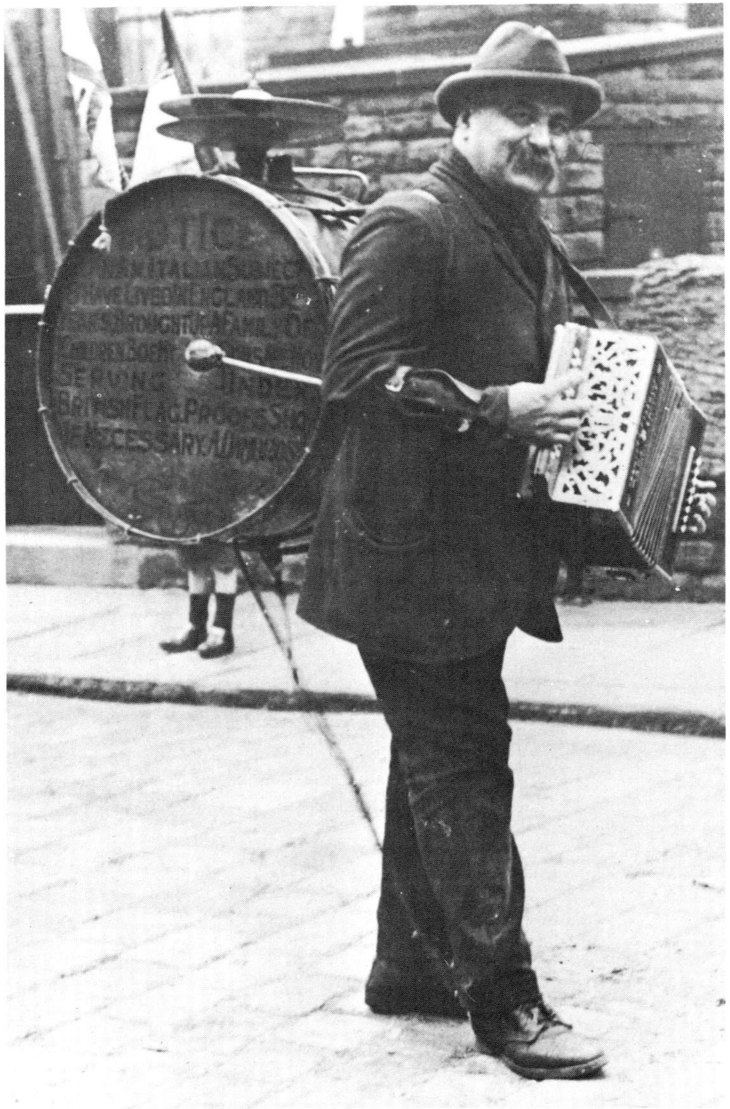

This one-man band was a familiar figure in Keighley streets during the First World War. The notice on his drum reads: "I am an Italian subject and have lived in England 35 years, brought up a family of children, 3 of my sons are now serving under British flag. Proofs shown if necessary. A. Dambros."

Another familiar old Keighley character, "Spud Mick", who sold roasted potatoes at the bottom of Cavendish Street.

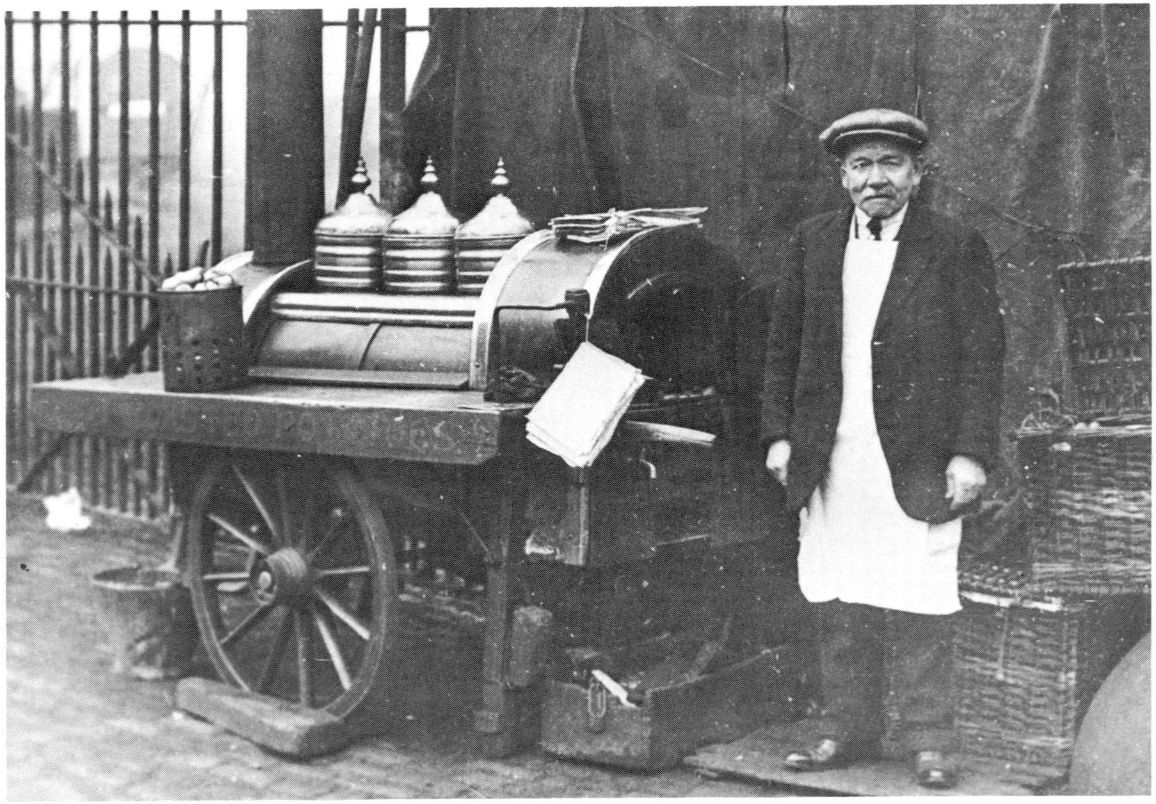

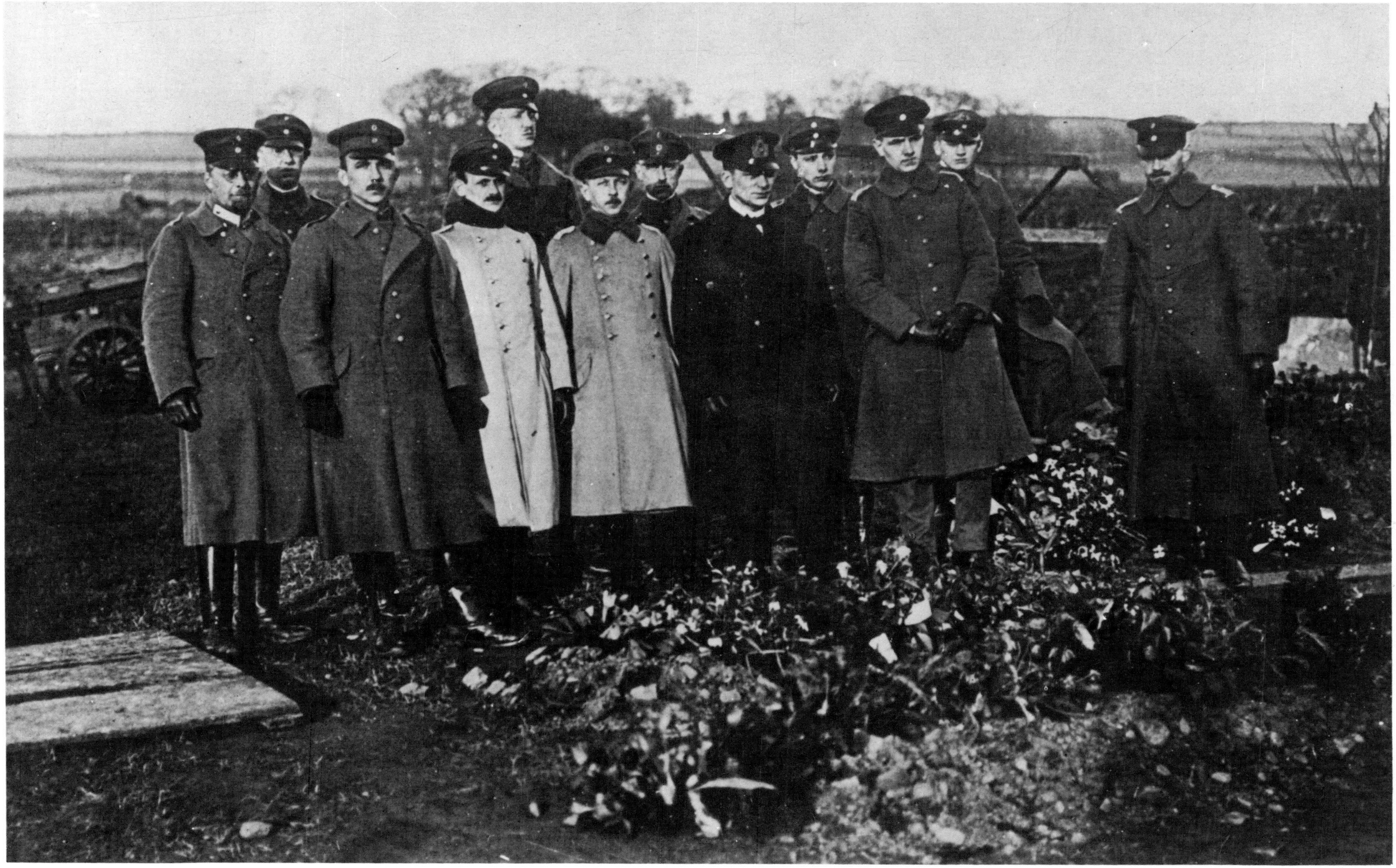

The influenza epidemic of 1919: German officer prisoners-of-war in Morton Cemetery, at their comrades' funeral. Keighley's German war graves would achieve a brief newsworthiness in 1936, when the Zeppelin "Hindenburg" dropped a crucifix over the town.

1920s advertising! Such was the reputation of "Ye Olde Shoppe" that this end of Cook Lane was known for decades as "Groves' Corner". Here, premises are emptying in preparation for demolition. This was part of the property bequeathed by John Drake in 1713 towards the upkeep of the Free Grammar School.

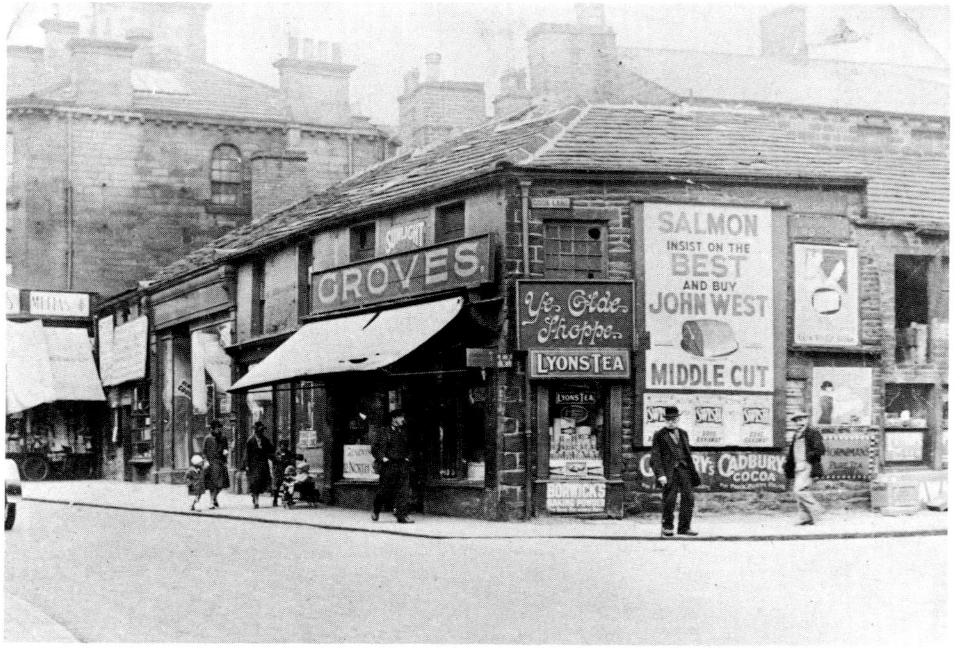

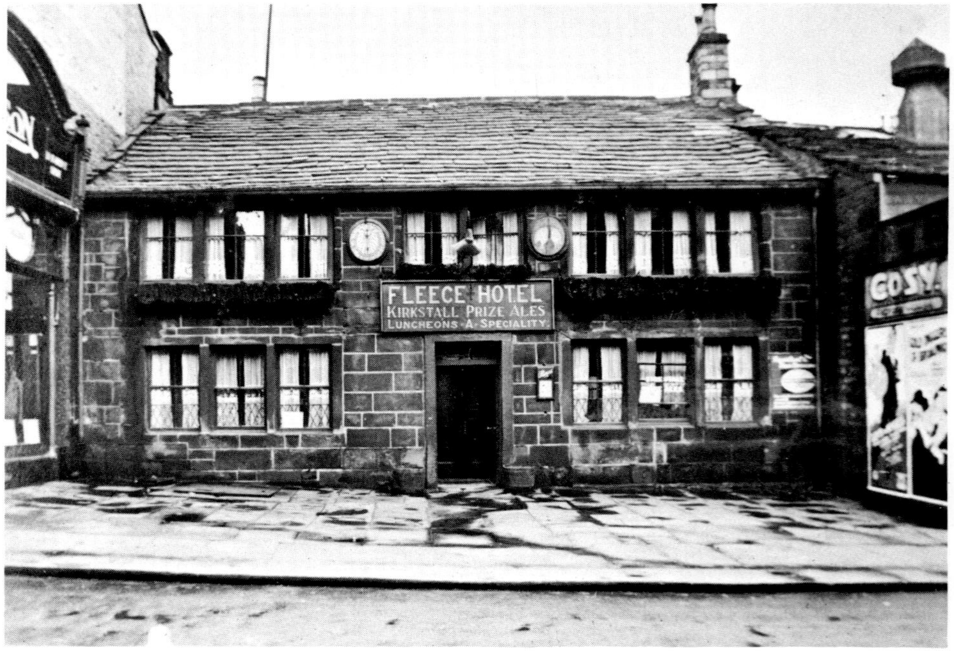

Of affectionate remembrance, the Fleece Inn, Low Street, demolished in 1935. From here, in the 1820s. the post coach "Royal Alexander" left for Leeds at seven o'clock every morning, Sundays excepted.

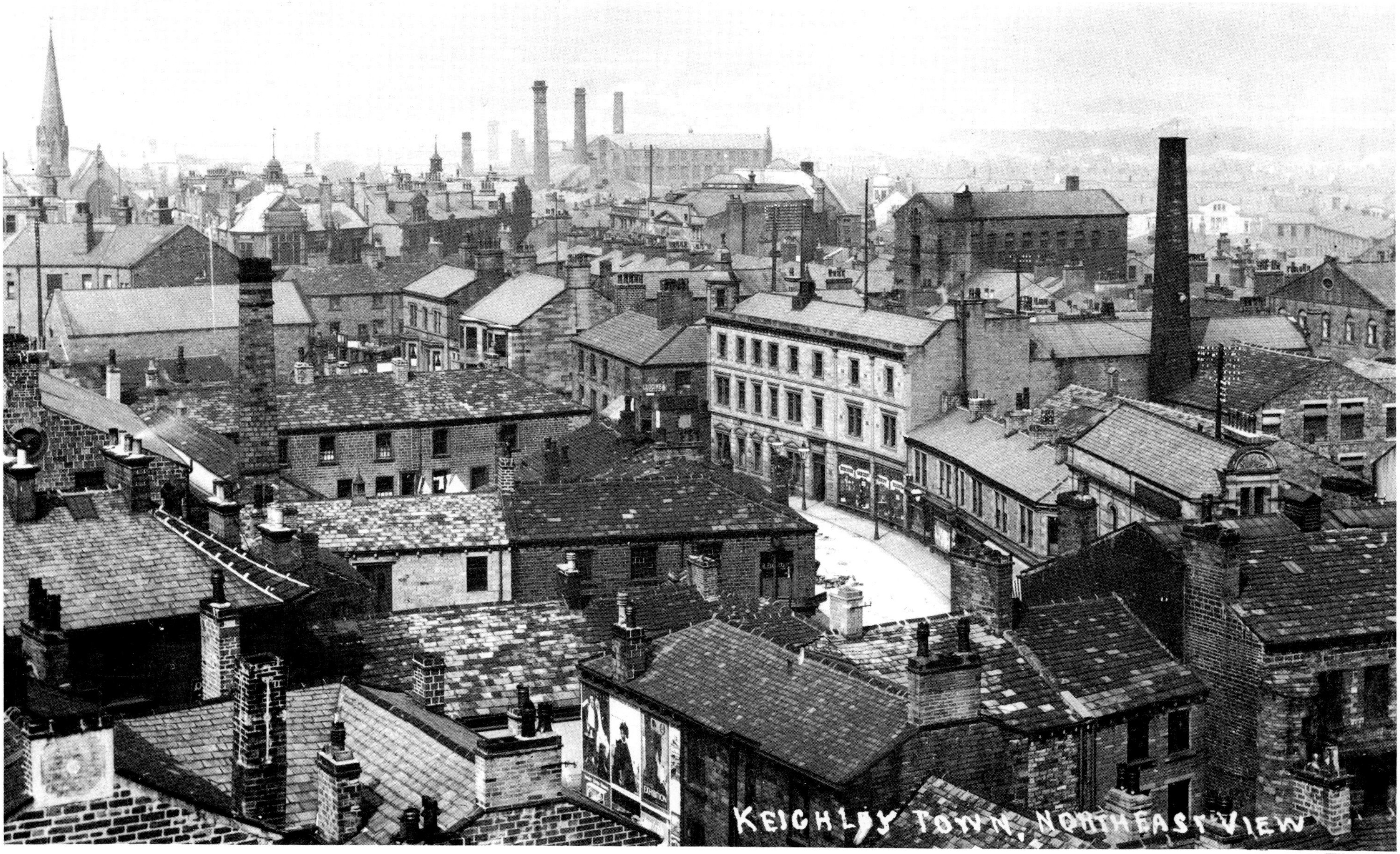

A bird's-eye view from Keighley Parish Church tower, half a century ago, across Cook Lane and, beyond, Townfield Gate. This area was almost wholly cleared to make way for the modern shopping centre and the Bus Station. Landmarks since demolished include, in the left background, the spire of the Cavendish Street United Methodist Free Church, and, in the middle background, the Hippodrome Theatre.

And finally, a photograph which spans a century and a half of Keighley's history: a water-wheel, symbol of the town's earlier industrial development, revealed during the between-the-wars clearances of slums spawned by the Industrial Revolution.

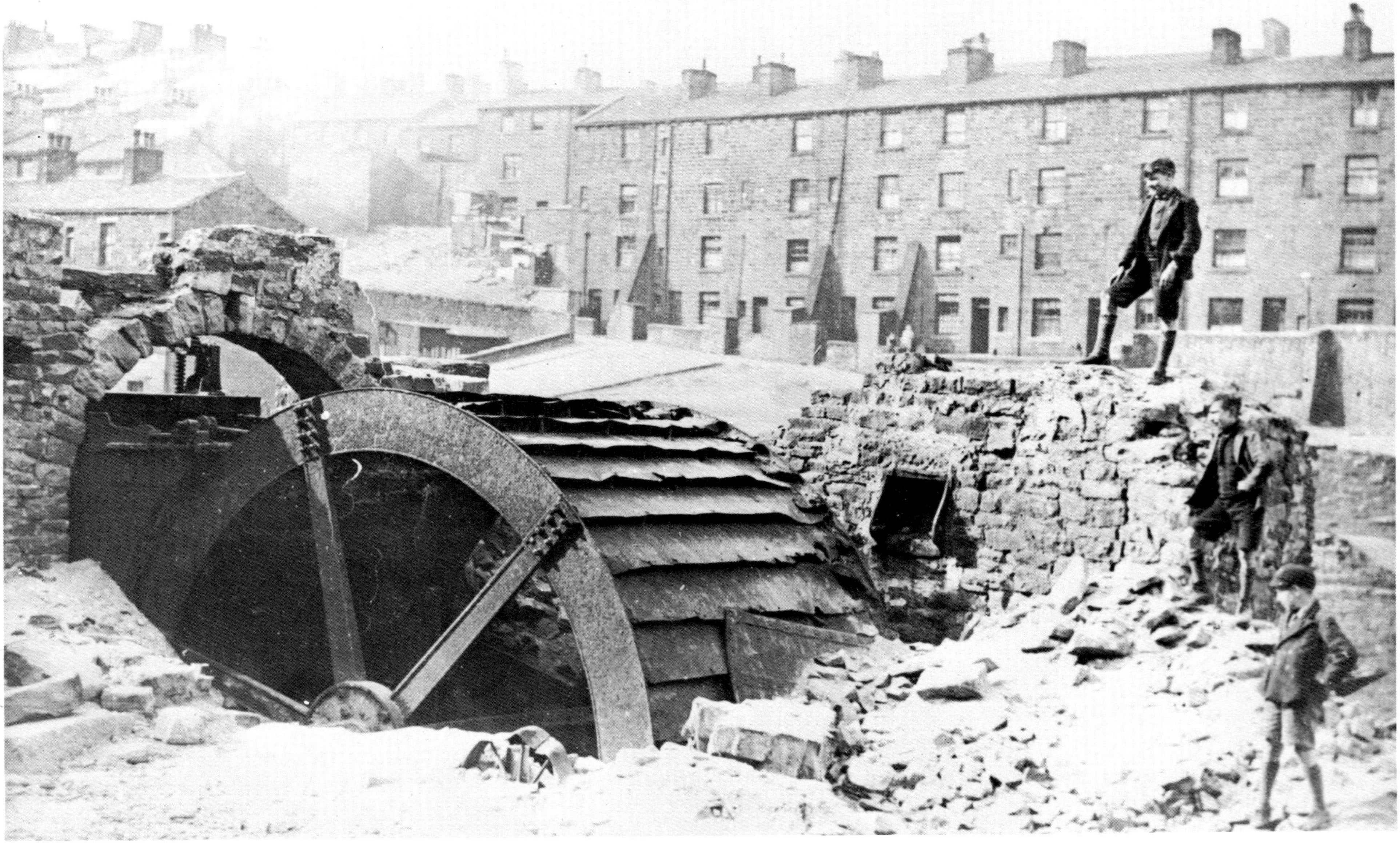